Handbook fc

American Bi

Cut Glass

Bill & Louise Boggess

Schiffer Publishing Ltd®

4880 Lower Valley Road, Atglen, PA 19310 USA

Dedicated
to those who helped us with information and photographs

"Who keeps the ability to see beauty never grows old."

Copyright © 2001 by Bill & Louise Boggess
Library of Congress Catalog Card Number: 00-106850

Designed by Bonnie M. Hensley
Type set in Americana XBd BT/Korinna BT

ISBN: 0-7643-1225-1
Printed in China
1 2 3 4

Published by Schiffer Publishing Ltd.
4880 Lower Valley Road
Atglen, PA 19310
Phone: (610) 593-1777; Fax: (610) 593-2002
E-mail: Schifferbk@aol.com
Please visit our web site catalog at **www.schifferbooks.com**

In Europe, Schiffer books are distributed by Bushwood Books
6 Marksbury Avenue Kew Gardens
Surrey TW9 4JF England
Phone: 44 (0) 20-8392-8585; Fax: 44 (0) 20-8392-9876
E-mail: Bushwd@aol.com
Free postage in the UK. Europe: air mail at cost.

This book may be purchased from the publisher.
Include $3.95 for shipping. Please try your bookstore first.
We are always looking for people to write books on new and related subjects.
If you have an idea for a book please contact us at the above address.
You may write for a free catalog.

Contents

Acknowledgments

We appreciated the following collectors who shared information and supplied pictures for this book: Joseph J. Ales, Antique Elegance, Bill Barnett, D. M. Berry, Howard & Patricia Blair, James & JoAnn Cozens, Maurice Crofford, Eric's Antiques, Bill Evans, Tommy de Graffenned, Phil & Karen Jarnagin, Jim Kimberline, Mrs. Margaret L. Lynn, Dow D. Mitchell, Ronald A. Noll, Suzanne Plunket, James Siri, Skinner's Auctions, Leroy C. Statt, and Phil Yonge.

A special "thank you" goes to Jeanne Brady, Sam & Becky Story, and Woody Auction for a large number of photographs; to Carol Weir and Walter Poeth for updating the value guide; to Glass Studio (Fred and Sharon Matthews) for special photographs on repairs.

We sincerely appreciate Peter B. Schiffer, our publisher, who suggested the title and encouraged us to continue working on the book in spite of delays, and our editor, Nancy Schiffer, who telephoned encouragement.

Finally, we thank the many who have bought our books on brilliant cut glass and continue to ask about the next one in spite of those delays.

Introduction

This Handbook endeavors to provide brief but simple answers to questions that arise when you buy or sell cut glass. The experienced collector can use this book to refresh a memory. The information offers a new collector or occasional purchaser help in buying. Finally, it provides quick research to dealers who buy and sell American brilliant cut glass.

For information about patterns or identifications we used interviews with retired elderly cutters, knowledgeable collectors, members of families who owned companies that produced this glass, well-informed dealers who sell cut glass. We have collected advertisements on cut glass from magazines published during the Brilliant Period and from current ones. We have purchased all books we could find written on cut glass. To the best of our knowledge this Handbook contains standard and special information on brilliant cut glass.

Our main sources of identification relied on original and reprinted catalogs of companies that produced cut glass. May this book help you find some good "buys" in American brilliant cut glass by taking it with you when you shop in person or use it when you check cut glass on the Internet at home.

The numbered illustration captions and the Value Guide in the Appendix of this book include letters that identify the *quality* of pieces in the photographs as follows:

S - for Standard
C - for Choice
P - for Premium
R - for Rare

Standard consists of a clear blank, simple pattern, and an ordinary shape.

Choice contains an ornate pattern, possibly a variance in shape, and the addition of a foot, handle or stopper.

Premium has an unusual shape and a very ornate pattern that entirely covers the blank.

Rare refers to special order or a museum-type piece. Knowing the characteristics of American cut glass will help you recognize a rare American piece from that produced by foreign companies.

Chapter 1
Characteristics of Cut Glass

On July 4, 1876, the United States opened the Centennial Exposition to the public in Philadelphia to celebrate 100 years as a nation. Exhibitors of cut glass, such as C. Dorflinger & Sons and Gillinder & Sons, decided to focus on ornate patterns everyone could learn to identify as American cut glass. Later the glass became known as American brilliant cut glass.

No one knows the exact origin of the term "brilliant." In 1950, M. Barrows & Company published AMERICAN CUT & ENGRAVED GLASS by Dorothy Daniel, a recognized authority. In the book she refers to cut glass produced in the United States after 1876, as "brilliant cut glass." No one knows if she originated the term, as she provided no reference. Certainly the phrase found ready acceptance everywhere.

American Features

From the beginning American companies found an abundance of pure-grained sand or silica relatively free of iron oxide. It aided American brilliant cut glass by containing the following features:

1. Brilliance Hold a piece of cut glass to any light and notice the refraction. The degree of refraction depends first on the amount of lead in the metal for blowing the glass. The Americans used a large amount as seen in this recipe from a small, typewritten booklet. William Gillinder highly recommended this particular one:

Sand...........................226 lbs.
Lead...........................224 lbs.
Ash.............................112 lbs.
Nitre...........................28 lbs
Arsenic.........................1 oz.
Maganese.......................2 oz.

The deep cutting of an ornate pattern (**C1**), the shape (**C2**) of the piece, and a thorough polishing removed any white marks from cutting the miters and also increased the brilliance.

2. Weight Along with the lead in the formula for blowing the blank, the thickness increased the weight (**P3**) of a piece of cut glass. Naturally, the weight varies with size and thickness of the blank (**C4**). You can easily test the heaviness by lifting the piece.

3. Sharpness Run your fingers over the pattern on the piece of cut glass and feel the sharpness. This sharpness resulted from the choice of motifs that formed the pattern, which covered the entire blank (**C5**). A thorough polishing further increased the sharpness of the pattern (**C6**). Any cutting on a cut glass blank turns white. Remember!

4. Ring An open piece of cut glass will ring when thumped lightly with your fingers or with the side of a pencil. The lead in the metal, the thickness of the blank, the size and depth of the shape determine the sound of the ring. Oddly, not all similar pieces ring with the same tone, not even those blown from the same metal.

Pieces of cut glass with a closed top, such as a decanter (**S7**) or a cologne (**C8**), will not ring. Always ask the owner of the piece to do the thumping. You may get a refusal. Rumor says that such thumping can break or fracture the glass. We have never talked to anyone who has witnessed such damage.

5. Function Companies produced cut glass for certain functions. A deep oval bowl the catalogs identified as used for fruit (**C9**). A shallow oval piece the catalog called a celery tray (**S10**). The company catalog usually indicated the function with the illustration.

6. Methods of Cutting After 1876, most American companies generally favored geometric patterns cut with a stone wheel, looking through the blank. To increase sales for brilliant cut glass, some companies turned to different methods of cutting. Charles Tuthill took the lead in intaglio, a reverse of cameo. First, he combined intaglio with geometric motifs (**C12**) and later focused only on intaglio fruit or flowers (**C13**).

H.P. Sinclaire, one of the first, engraved shapes with copper wheel cutting of flowers (**S14**) and of scenes (**C15**). Later T.G. Hawkes and others also engraved scenes. To engrave, the cutter used small copper wheels and worked from the top of the blank under a water-dripping funnel. Etching resulted from the application of acid to a waxed blank.

When these new patterns did not increase sales, some companies used figured blanks (**S16**) that decreased the value of the piece. The craftsman blew the blank into a mold that contained part of the pattern. The worker cut only the motifs, such as flowers. A large company polished the molded parts. Finally companies decided to return to old type cutting. Unfortunately, before companies could revive heavy cutting, World War 1 started. Lead so essential to cut glass went to war. When the War ended, companies already used thin-cut blanks for engraving or etching.

Features of Foreign Cut Glass

In the past and the present, foreign companies frequently copied American brilliant cut glass. An unsuspecting dealer may buy foreign glass and sell it as American. By comparing foreign glass to American, you can often avoid buying it.

1. Brilliance The metal formula for blowing cut glass does not contain as much lead as that of the American formula; hence it lacks brilliance provided by this ingredient. If you place a foreign piece beside the same shape in American cut glass, you can usually see the difference in brilliance. The simple motifs that form the basic pattern of foreign pieces either old or new lack the ornate patterns of American glass. Note this present-day lamp by the Yasemin Cut Glass Company (**C17**).

2. Weight The lack of lead and the thin blank (**C18**) of this company lacks American heaviness. This vase signed Yegemi adds some weight with size (**C19**).

3. Sharpness With a thin blank, the cuts for the design have a shallowness, which often you can see.

The design of a pattern the foreign company greatly simplifies (**S20**) and (**S21**). Particularly note the difference of the foreign motifs from American ones or in the variance of the pointed rim by the foreign piece (**S22**).

4. Ring Because of the formula for the metal in blowing and the thin blank, the ring has a flat tone. If you think a foreign company produced the item, ask the owner to thump it.

5. Function The foreign companies cut pieces with the same basic functions as those of the Americans, such as bowls, celery, trays, or vases. This makes separating the foreign from the American glass somewhat difficult by function.

6. Method of Cutting The modern cut glass increases production with a diamond wheel. These wheels, embedded with industrial diamonds, cut 10 to 20 times faster than by the older American method.

Foreign Companies

The number of foreign companies regularly producing cut glass similar to that of American has increased rapidly over the years.

1. England This country early produced cut glass using simple motifs for patterns that covered very little of the blank. During recessions, some of their cutters early came to the United States and secured work cutting their simple patterns. In England especially you can find old and modern cut glass.

2. France As a competitor of England, France early produced cut glass. They frequently held conventions displaying their glass. They still cut glass today.

3. Germany For years old German cut glass sold extensively in the United States. In fact some American cut glass companies imitated the glass in the early years.

4. Sweden This country early produced cut glass and continues in the present.

5. Japan This country has recently entered the field of cutting. A collector bought a bowl in Japan very cheaply. When she examined it after arriving home, she found the etched signature, "Japan."

6. Israel Several collectors have bought cut glass in this area.

Also, The Yasemin Cut Glass Company in Colorado Springs, Colorado, offers pieces signed or unsigned at a lesser price. A factory located on the border in **Turkey** supposedly produces the glass. Some pieces copy the shapes and designs of American cut glass closely, while other shapes differ slightly. The company uses several types of rims: an uncut scalloped one, a round smooth one, a rounded saw-tooth one that copies American glass. If you write the company, it will send you information.

Carefully examine the cut glass you already own by applying these characteristics for American and foreign cut pieces. You may recognize some items you own as produced by foreign companies. Since American cut glass has the greater value, you may want to get rid of the foreign pieces. You can sell, trade, or use as gifts. When you decide to buy more cut glass, use these features to determine whether produced by American companies or imitations done by a foreign company. Concentrate on American cut glass for a better investment.

C1 A 9-inch bowl with geometric hobstars as the dominant motifs.

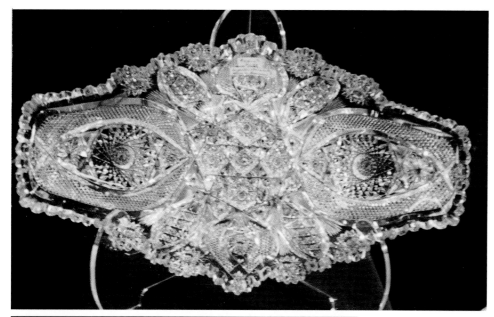

C2 An 18-inch tray with an unusual shape and ornate pattern of framed hobstars.

P3 A footed cake tray (9 1/4-inches tall and 15-1/2 inches in diameter) shows heaviness in a piece of cut glass.

C5 A sharply, ornate pattern that covers the entire blank of the carafe with geometric motifs.

C4 A butter tub with a 5 1/2-inch diameter and pinwheel motifs has a thick blank.

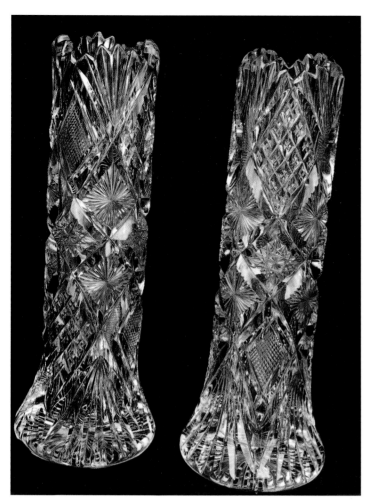

C6 Two hatpin holders, 9-inches in height, illustrate sharpness with simple geometric motifs.

C8 This stoppered cologne will not ring when thumped.

S7 The stopper in the whiskey decanter will not let the piece ring.

C9 A 9-inch oval bowl the catalog identified as "for fruit."

C11 A 12-inch round vase cut with hobstars and flat stars.

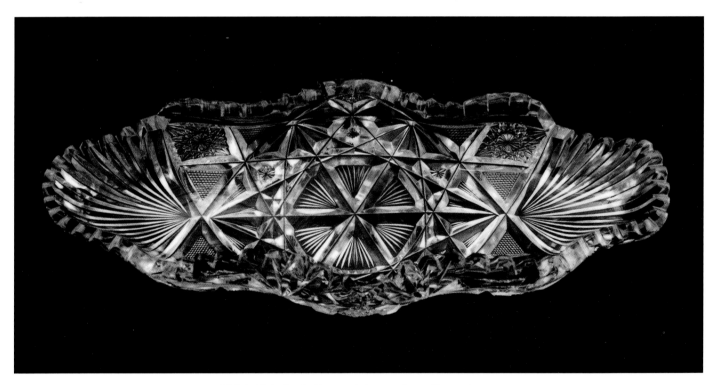

S10 A 13-inch, shallow oval the catalog calls a celery.

C12 On this 7-inch, square tray Charles Tuthill cut a hobstar border around the flowers.

S14 H. P. Sinclaire cut a geometric center with a floral border and called the pattern on this bonbon Versailles & Engraving.

P13 For this large bowl Tuthill used only intaglio flowers.

C15 A 9-inch plate Sinclaire cut a scene with a floral border.

S16 A 8-inch jug cut on a figured blank.

C17 A 22-inch lamp produced by Yasemin Cut Glass Company in a shop on the Turkish border today.

C18 A punch bowl 13-inches tall produced by the Yasemin Cut Glass Company lack the shape and weight of an American one.

S20 A foreign company greatly simplified the swirl pattern with the motifs on the curved panels.

C19 A foreign produced vase, 13-inches tall, and signed Yegemi has a thin blank and motifs slightly different from American ones.

S21 A decanter in a simple pattern typical of modern patterns today.

S22 The rim and the motifs on this vase indicate foreign production.

Chapter 2
The Search For Cut Glass

The computer offers sources of locating cut glass without leaving your home. We made the mistake of buying the cheaper word processor instead of the more costly and complicated computer. If you own a computer, most likely, you have already used it for research on cut glass. Anyone buying cut glass, however, can use these tested methods for locating pieces you want to buy. Begin your search for cut glass by checking the yellow pages of your telephone directory under the heading of "Antiques." Make a list of shops. Look for a location with several shops near each other.

Established Markets

An established market operates at a specific location during regular or advertised business hours. These markets include individual shops, collectives, antiques shows, and large flea markets. The ones that specialize in selling cut glass offer the most choices in size (**S23**), shapes or patterns. Those that handle only a limited number of pieces, such as bowls or sugar and cream (**C24**), sell what they can find or favor small shapes. The last group does not handle cut glass, but they can recommend shops that do.

1. Individual Shop You want to visit regularly or when convenient, a shop that specializes in selling cut glass and make friends with the owner. Mention some special item you want for your collection.

2. Collective A collective consists of a number of antiques dealers who rent a space in a large building to display and sell their wares. You want to make an effort to know the owner of the collective and explain your interest in cut glass. Do make friends with any dealer who sells cut glass.

The collective follows a time schedule, so one dealer may depend on a nearby one to manage a display and make sales one day a week so the owner can search for replacements. All items carry a price tag, and you pay at the entry desk. If you visit the collective periodically, you'll find cut glass as well as other interesting antiques.

3. Antiques Shows Large antique shows include cut glass dealers. Most big shows follow a basic schedule for spring, summer, and fall. You can see the schedule advertised in the newspaper or antiques magazines. Dealers who specialize in cut glass offer the greatest choices. Dealers who stock only a few pieces such as a vase (**S25**) frequently offer bargains.

4. Large Flea Markets Some geographical areas may sponsor a large flea market on a certain date each month. The dealers usually occupy the same spaces, so you will know where to find the ones you want to see.

Markets with Changing Schedules

Some markets may open on any date. You often find what appear bargains in cut glass until you note the need for costly repair.

1. Small Flea Market If you check the flea market section in a large weekend newspaper, you may find a notice. Sometimes the person who runs the flea market will arrange to send notices to individuals in adjacent areas. Ask your friends for information on these flea markets. You can find most any type of cut glass pieces, from small to large. The owner buys the available at the affordable price.

2. House or Estate Sales The heirs of a deceased collector may hire a professional to handle a clearance sale in the home itself. The person handling the sale will thoroughly advertise the date and time. The items for sale usually consist of pieces a collector will own as a celery (**C26**) or a jug (**C27**). The items for sale generally contain a price tag. As time passes without a sale, you will note a mark down. Talk to the person in charge and ask for a notice on the next sale.

3. Garage Sales To find information on garage sales, check the local newspaper under antiques or collectives for location. If you can call ahead, ask about cut glass. Such a call can save you time and travel. At the garage sale always ask the person in charge about other pieces of cut glass. At such a sale we asked about other pieces. The owner went into the house and brought out a vase (**S28**) she sold us.

4. Church Bazaars The larger churches usually have a room reserved for donations from members. The bazaar may open on weekends or at announced dates to sell items. Periodically during the year the church will hold a large weekend bazaar. Expect to find a matching nice piece or matching tumbler (**C29**) to complete your set. Do get acquainted with the persons who handle these bazaars and volunteer to help with them. Frankly explain that you collect cut glass but feel you can help with the bazaars.

5. Auctions Large auctions generally advertise available items of cut glass, as a cologne (**C30**). Most pieces come under the heading of large or rare. The advanced publicity can help you decide if you want to attend. The company in charge of the auction may offer four to six small pieces in one box at a single price. Bid on this. You can keep what you want and sell the others to pay the total cost.

Some auctions specialize in the selling of cut glass from a personal collection. These auctions often publish a catalog picturing the outstanding pieces and permit you to send in a bid for a small charge. In some cases you later can buy a list of prices paid for the items. This pricing can give you an idea of a basic value for individual pieces. Again, the price may depend on whether several collectors of cut glass attend and run up the bidding. Small, local auctions may prove more productive than the larger ones, but they lack the extensive choices offered by national ones.

Personal Contact

Nothing substitutes for personal contacts, especially of letting others know that you collect cut glass. Displaying your collection at a museum or library will also spark interest from buyers or collectors.

1. Friends and Neighbors From time to time remind friends and neighbors you collect cut glass. Ask them occasionally if they have met any person with cut glass. When you meet new people, mention about your collecting in the conversation. The result will surprise you. A new acquaintance brought a nun to our home. She had inherited a few pieces of cut glass including a pair of candlestick holders (**C31**). We bought all the pieces so she could make a donation to a cause she supported.

2. Advertising Contacts You may contact a person who advertises cut glass for sale under "classified" in an antiques magazine. With one person we became long distance friends and bought her glass and that of her friend.

3. Dealers One day in mid-afternoon the telephone rang, and a male voice gave me the name of the person who suggested he contact us about the sale of some cut glass he bought from the owner of a house he sold. He wanted to know if we would like to see the pieces. When I asked him to set a date, he explained that he talked on his car telephone right in front of our home and could bring the pieces inside. We bought the four pieces of cut glass, including a footed bowl (**C32**). We suggested he contact us again when he found other pieces. He became one of our best suppliers.

4. Clubs and Organizations At an antiques glass club, both local and national, you will meet knowledgeable collectors. Some may have duplicates to sell or exchange

for a piece you own. Working with these collectors will help you locate other markets.

Bill, my husband, started a conversation at a men's luncheon club with a person whose wife died recently. The individual explained he bought an apartment in a health center. His children took what they wanted of the furniture, and then he sold the house. None of the children wanted the cut glass because of the "don't touch" memory. Bill offered to send him some dealers who might buy it. He promised to let Bill know. Several meetings later he told Bill that he packed the glass in two boxes and put them in the trunk of his car. After the meeting they went to his car. He insisted that Bill accept sixteen boxed pieces of cut glass as a gift so that it would have a good home. Among the 12 pieces, we found two champagne tumblers (**C33**).

When I substituted in a bridge club, and I mentioned my cut glass collecting, one of the women told me about her neighbor trying to sell an étagère filled with it at the price set by the person handling the estate. We bought the glass and prepared to leave. The woman reminded us that the prices included the "stand," and she insisted that we take the valuable étagère.

5. The Unexpected The newly married daughter and husband of a neighbor bought an old house to update. The heir asked them to haul some boxes of "stuff" to the dump for him. They decided to look inside the boxes before carrying them to the dump. When they opened the large boxes, they found a set of fine old china, pieces of art glass and some cut glass.

I mentioned at a class I taught at the local college for senior citizens about collecting cut glass. At the next meeting of the class, one of the members brought me two pieces, a vase (**S34**) and a bowl she bought for ten dollars from a neighbor. I insisted on paying her more, but she sternly refused.

Another friend who knew we collected cut glass told us about seeing some in a shop that sold antiques furniture. We went at once and bought the cut glass he displayed. Now the owner calls us when he gets any cut glass.

Individual Ingenuity

With a little thought and planning, you can find cut glass available in a number of locations.

1. A Walk A dealer told us how he found cut glass for his shop. On a sunny Saturday or Sunday afternoon, he walked through neighborhoods that contained old Victorian homes. When he saw anyone watering the yard or sitting on the front porch, he stopped and asked if they owned any cut glass they wanted to sell. They almost automatically said "No." He asked about a recent appraisal, then offered to give them one free. He gave them a dealer's evaluation and picked out several pieces he wanted to buy. He wrote the prices on a sheet of paper they furnished him and gave them his card in case they decided to sell them. He thanked them for a pleasant visit. He said they rarely waited a week before they offered to sell.

2. Planned Vacations A collector checked out the small towns on her vacation drive. If the area published a weekly newspaper, she advertised on the front page—if possible—where anyone who wanted to sell American cut glass could reach her at a local motel on certain dates. She said this worked very well for cut glass and inspired her to learn the basics of other antiques. The owners brought in not only cut glass but also china and pottery.

3. Highway Signs A couple that traveled a country road frequently to visit relatives became attracted to a small store that advertised antique farm equipment. A pair of red flannel underwear flapped on a flagpole in the front to attract attention. They decided to stop and see if the owner displayed other antiques. He did! They bought his entire stock of cut glass: a spoon holder, a hatpin holder, and a cologne bottle in Hob Diamond cut by Dorflinger (**C35**).

With a little planning and imagination you can find places to buy American brilliant cut glass. Always carry a notebook with you to jot down the location of places where you found cut glass and comment on the selection as to excellent, good, or fair. In the future, make a point of visiting these locations again.

S23 A flower center in a simple pattern with a flat star as dominate motif.

S25 Most dealers have one or more vases.

C24 An ornate pattern with a hobstar motif in a sugar and cream.

C26 A 12-inch celery with a flashed hobstar as the dominant motif.

C27 A 7-inch jug with a flashed single star as dominant motif.

S28 A 10-inch vase with bulbous base and flared top.

18

S29 A water tumbler with a hobstar motif.

C30 A cologne with a facet cut stopper.

C31 A pair of tall candlestick holders.

19

C32 A footed cut glass bowl with 16-point hobstars.

C33 Two champagne tumblers in different patterns.

S34 A cup type vase with a hobstar motif, foot, and knob.

C35 A cologne in Hob Diamond by C. Dorflinger or Hobnail by T. G. Hawkes.

Chapter 3
Sources of Information

A beautiful piece of cut glass (**C36**) you bought inspired you to search for information, but you need to know where to begin. Within recent years we have compiled and classified the following sources for information on American brilliant cut glass.

Published Records

Many printed records have become available in recent years to anyone who seeks them. Only you know the information you want, but possibly you need help on how to contact the sources. Determine what you need to know and utilize this information to help locate the best records for your research.

1. Company Catalogs In recent years old catalogs have surfaced from attics, basements, or personal estate papers. Both individuals and organizations now reprint these old catalogs and sell them to people who buy cut glass. The more catalogs you own, the more identifications you can make.

Gaps in dates appear frequently. A company may repeat popular patterns in later catalog issues but in different shapes. Catalogs offer an excellent method of identification.

2. Patent Records The records provide a number, the name of the person applying, the company assigned, the date, serial number, and term of the patent on the "glass dish" (**C37**). A patent on cut glass lasted from three to five years approximately. Unfortunately the change of a minor motive could break the patent. Companies did not patent all the pieces they produced but mostly the outstanding ones.

A legal association may have copies of the patent records in your area. Contact the reference librarian at your local library or a lawyer about the location. This office has a copy machine you may use at the standard price. Otherwise you can go to the patent office in Washington, D.C. and make copies of any records on cut glass. You'll find the information listed in the index under glass dish or object. Check to see if the listing mentioned cut glass. Compare the copies you make to illustrations in old catalogs. Availability and lack of information make patent records a poor source for researching identification.

3. Advertisements Women's magazines of the cut glass period often picture a piece and give the pattern name and company that produced it. Some libraries have a special stack of old magazines. Check the libraries near you to find out if any have these magazines. Make a copy of any advertisements that picture the piece, name the pattern and the producer.

4. Antiques Magazines Current magazines on antiques you often can find at the library. If not, why not subscribe to one or more. Send for a copy to determine if you want to subscribe. Read every article. See if you can find any information that does not seem accurate and compare these facts to another source.

5. Auction Catalogs The large auction companies often publish a list of cut glass for sale and picture many large pieces such as a flower center (**S38**) or a smaller one as a cologne (**S39**). Pattern identification or signature when known appears in the information. You may find one of your items pictured. If you can't attend the auction, you can order a selling price list for a small sum. Knowing the current prices may help you judge the value of your pieces or what you will pay for a similar item. At an auction so much depends on whether a number of collectors attend and bid up the price as for a heavily cut celery (**C40**).

6. News Letter A number of clubs print a newsletter, which you receive if you belong. The American Cut Glass Association publishes a ten-month publication for its members. Sometimes clubs send their publications to large libraries. Your local library can give you this information.

7. Books on Cut Glass By all means check the date of publication on any book about American brilliant cut glass. Old catalogs now available will refute improvised names of patterns. The American Cut Glass Association recently started work on improvised pattern names and will try to supply the catalog one if available. Avoid confusion and use the name in the catalog or leave the piece unidentified. These writers did the best they could with lack of reference material and the demands of collectors for a name. Your library can always secure these older books on library loan. You only pay the postage. We depend on two experts for the following information.

The Internet

Any discussion about research on American cut glass must include the Internet. When you own a computer, you probably already know how to use it for research. Perhaps you use the computer at the local library, and an employee there will assist you in doing research. If you plan to buy a computer, try to get instruction on how to do research.

You will find many ways and sources to discover the available information. No one source will do it all. Begin your search with American Cut Glass Association web page *(WWW.cutglass.org)* which contains information about the Association, pictures of cut glass, and links to interesting Web Sites.

Additional avenues to pursue include search engines, such as Alta Vista, Web Crawler, Yahoo, and others. Begin by typing "American brilliant cut glass" in quotation marks on the search box, and you will find many Web Sites to explore. If you fail to use quotation marks, the information search becomes too broad, or you will find too much information about other topics besides cut glass.

The Internet provides a researcher's dream to supplement information on American brilliant cut glass. Of course, nothing can replace looking and touching the real piece. By all means do take advantage of this modern-day research source.

Institutions

Most of these institutions have a research librarian who can provide you with information. Do send a photograph or professional drawing that shows the pattern, and include a self-addressed, stamped envelope.

1. Libraries The reference librarian proves most helpful in locating special material for you. Do make friends with this person and explain the information you need. Check the public one, that of a nearby college, or the Library of Congress.

2. Museums Most museums have a research librarian or a specialist to help you secure information. Those that display cut glass do have microfiche of old catalogs you can buy. You will need to use the special machine for printing the film. Most libraries have these machines.

The following museums have done much research on American cut glass: Libbey in Ohio, Corning in New York, and Lightner in Florida. The Florida museum has devoted a room to displaying American cut glass. We have found all most cooperative in sending us information and pattern identifications.

Don't overlook small museums. They may have the very special information you can't find elsewhere. Your local librarian can possibly give you a list of those near you.

3. Silver Companies These companies added silver to cut glass pieces at a company's request. A syrup pitcher gets a silver rim, handle and attached lid (**S41**). A silver lid fits on a puff box (**S42**); a silver foot forms the base of a vase (**S43**). Silver went on jugs, bowls, and punch bowls to guard against chipping. Usually the silver carried the name or the trademark of the company and type of silver. Sterling on the silver raised the value more than plate.

During the years one company bought out another. The reference librarian can help you with the ones still in business or those bought by larger ones. Most of the present-day companies have a reference librarian where you may secure identifications from the files of a company sold. You may get charged a fee for such information.

4. United States Agencies The Library of Congress and the Patent Office have a few old catalogs in their files. You may write and ask them about the old cut glass catalogs. They will send such catalogs on library loan. You must use them in your library, but you pay only the cost of the postage.

Contact with Experts

Possibly your best source of research consists of contact with people who have done research on cut glass.

1. Members of Antiques Clubs At the library you can get information on the various antiques clubs in your area and their officers. Visit the club, but call the president and get permission. Explain that you may want to join. Meet the people interested in cut glass. They, too, want information on cut glass as much as you do. A visit to a club and meeting the members can help you decide if you want to join and share your common interest.

2. Professional Speakers Club members hire professional speakers, so you have an opportunity to make a date with them later. Naturally you will pay for the personal conference. If you join a national organization, you will have more possibilities of speaking personally with the speakers. The national organization usually holds a yearly convention. Chapters of the organization also hold district meetings. These offer you contact with experts who speak on cut glass.

Get acquainted with these sources of information. Some of these resources may lead you to others. Always stay aware to any possibility that may alert you to new information. Those who buy or collect cut glass willingly tell others or exchange this information.

P36 A 12-inch tray with large hobstars and flashed fans.

C37 A copy of a cut glass dish from the Patent Records.

P38 A large flower center with decorated handles.

S39 A cologne bottle with hobstars separated by parallel miters.

S42 A puff box with a decorated silver lid.

S43 An engraved vase with a silver base signed Gorham.

C40 A 12-inch celery with an elaborate pattern that contains hobstars as the dominant motif.

S41 A typical syrup pitcher with silver appointments.

Chapter 4
Identification Clues

Each time you buy a new piece of cut glass, examine it carefully. See if you can recognize any part of the pattern, such as the outline, the motifs, or any combination. Any recognition you give a piece of cut glass can increase the value or possibly lead you to the name of the pattern or the company that produced it. Begin your analysis with an examination of the pieces you already own.

Single Features

Start any examination of a piece by looking for single features.

1. Labels Some companies, such as Dorflinger, used paper labels. Naturally, the buyer removed these when using the piece. Later before the company closed, John Dorflinger, a relative, took over the management and printed duplicates of these labels he placed on pieces he identified as cut by the company. In the glass room at the White House we saw these printed labels displayed on pieces used by various presidents. Don't expect to find pieces with original labels.

2. Signatures Glass companies placed the name of the company or a symbol on a rubber stamp, dipped it in acid, and pressed it against the blank. At first companies signed only the outstanding pieces, but around 1900 Hawkes and Libbey advertised they signed all pieces; however some slipped by without a signature.

At times you find fake signatures on pieces of cut glass. A man in Southern California contacted dealers and offered to sign pieces. Some fakers use an electric needle, so you can feel the signature. You cannot feel an acid etched one. Sometimes these fake signatures may not duplicate the original ones as shown in the appendix of this book. We found a block printed Hawkes on a modern shaped basket.

Knowing where companies usually placed a signature may simplify finding them. On a rounded piece, such as a bowl or nappy, the acid signature generally went on the inside center. J. Hoare signed a little off center. At times Libbey placed the signature below the top rim on the inside. Some companies placed the signature on the outer rim or the base of a bowl, decanter, or jug.

With a footed piece, the signature may appear near the edge on the top or under the foot. On a handled piece you can locate the signature directly under the handle or on an oval space on top of the handle.

A jug may have the signature on the outer or inner lip. A covered bonbon may place the signature on the inside center of the lid and base or both. We owned a covered bonbon for several years before we found the Tuthill signature on the flat top of the rim on both pieces. Do search the ordinary places for a signature before you look for the unusual ones.

3. Silver Additions Beginning in the 1890s, glass companies began to add silver to cut glass pieces. Simple addition included stoppers (**S44**), (**S45**), and (**S46**). A silver lid went on a puff box (**S47**), but one company matched an ornate design with a combination ornate lid and knob on a cigar jar (**R48**). A silver rim circled the low bowl (**S49**). Plain hinged rims went on jewel boxes (**C50**) and (**C51**), on glove boxes (**S52**) and (**S53**), and on a handkerchief box (**S54**).

Spouts on jugs (**C55**) and (**C56**), rims on vases (**C57**), and handles and rim on a loving cup (**R58**) greatly increased the value. Companies added silver for candles on candelabras (**R59**) and (**R60**). No doubt you can find other pieces with the addition of silver. Do look on the silver for the hallmark or the name of the company. At most libraries you can find a book of silver hallmarks by companies. If your library does not have one, arrange to get the book by library loan. When you identify the hallmark, check to see if the company operates today or if it sold to a present one and contact it for information.

4. Liners Some pieces of cut glass, as a fern, have a metal liner. The liner may carry the name of the company that produced it. Some companies specialized in making liners, so you may secure information from them if still in business. If sold, the company that bought it may still have the files. By checking different references, you may discover what glass companies bought from the one producing the liner.

5. Combination of Minor Motifs Companies combined several minor motifs to form a link between dominant ones. Hawkes repeated the double fans in several patterns with different dominant motifs and identified them as different patterns. Quaker City (**C61**) used double diamonds between the clusters of hobstars in Columbia Pattern and with other dominant motifs. Hoare pattern #1397 (**C62**) combined a fan and star he used in several patterns. An unidentified comport combines four minor motifs that link the hobstars (**C63**). Libbey also repeated the same combination of minor motifs in a connecting device as in this comport in pattern #55 (**S64**). Look for the above features on the cut glass you already own or that you plan to buy.

Pattern Analysis

Before you buy more pieces of cut glass, examine the ones you own and apply these steps. A pattern consists of a miter outline, dominant motifs, and minor ones or combinations that unite the cutting.

1. Miter Outline The master craftsman sketched or partially cut a pattern on a blank. The rougher took the illustration and cut the miter outline on a blank. He may change the outline slightly to fit the shape of the blank. The miter outlines started simply in the early years but gradually became more complicated. The more ornate the outline, the higher the value and the price.

Bars Parallel miters formed intersecting bars that framed the motifs (**S65**).

Rows The rows formed by the miters frequently ran parallel (**C66**).

Border and Miters The rougher cut plain parallel or notched miters but left space at the top or top and bottom for a geometric border (**S67**).

Star The points of a large center star extended almost to the rim. Motifs occupied the space between or within the points (**C68**).

Gothic Arch Two miters met to form a pointed arch at the top and sometimes at both the top and near the center (**P69**).

Panels Parallel miters formed the spaces for repetitive motifs (**C70**).

Swirls The craftsman replaced the parallel miters with spinning ones filled with repetitive motifs (**P71**).

Pointed Loops The miters circled the dominant motifs and used minor ones to unite the pattern (**C72** and **C73**).

Combinations The artistic rougher met the customers demand for more ornate cut glass by combination of panels and rows (**C74**) and panels and loops (**P75**).

2. The Motifs When the rougher completed the miter outline, the smoother removed any roughness and added the decorative motifs. The motifs in a pattern included one or perhaps two dominant motifs. The minor motifs enhanced the major one, such as fan between the star prongs (**C76**) or at the end (**C77**).

3. Units The major and minor motifs combined to form units the pattern repeated (**C78**). The number of units and the arrangement depended on the size and shape of the piece of glass.

4. Polisher The American blanks turned white when cut, so they needed polishing to maintain the brilliance. This craftsman used wooden or felt wheels to remove this whiteness after he dusted the piece of glass with a mixture of pomice and rottenstone and permitted water from above to drip on it.

With the rising cost of producing cut glass, companies turned to acid bath which worked faster in removing the whiteness, especially for detailed heavy cuts. The workman covered any part of the blank not cut with wax. He placed the item in a wire basket and dipped it into the acid bath. If not correctly mixed and timed, the acid made wavy lines on the clear miters. Often the large companies gave a slight buffing to a piece after an acid bath. In a small company one man performed all of these steps. Women washed the cut glass and stored if for sale.

Slight Alterations in Patterns

The late Bill Iorio taught us to recognize a pattern with slight alterations. He drew a sketch of a flat tray on a piece of paper and then wrapped it about a round piece. He pointed out where minor motifs would need changing. He also explained why two identical patterns used a different major motif. "The buyer may want a pinwheel rather than a hobstar. So we made the change to get a sale."

1. Site A tall tubular vase would need to repeat the unit three times (**C79**). The cutter needed minor motifs to unite the units. On a bowl a combination motif united the four hobstars unit (**C80**). A flat-shaped decanter would need only two units. As you look at pieces of cut glass, count the number of units that comprise the pattern.

You may used the number of units to compare the design to a photograph in a book, antiques magazine, or an illustration in a company catalog. Once you identify this unit, you can then check the miter outline and the special motifs in the pattern.

2. Shape You can see the need to change minor motifs to fit a round, square, or oval shape. The cutter endeavored to keep the major motifs the same. With a little observation, you see the need to change minor motifs or even eliminate them. Even with a slight change, you hardly notice it.

3. Popular Patterns A company may take a popular pattern that sells exceptionally and change only the dominant motif but leave the rest of the pattern the same. Hoare did this frequently by substituting another dominate motif.

Hawkes cut Brunswick with two borders but renamed the pattern Marquis. When a craftsman left a company, he received permission to take the patterns he created with him. Singleton cut Brunswick Pattern but called it Westminster.

4. Traveling Craftsmen Craftsmen proved notorious in changing jobs from company to company. If not permitted to take the patterns they cut, they made only slight changes. In some patterns they made no changes at all but gave the piece a different name. So you will find several companies cutting the same pattern and under the same name or different one.

5. Patent Breaking To break a patent, the craftsman could change one motif and create a new pattern. When you match the piece to an illustration in a catalog except for one motif, you may suspect a broken patent.

6. Buyer's Request A buyer may request the change of a dominant motif as previously mentioned.

So use these suggestions to help you with identifications and exceptions found in patterns.

S45 An ink well with a decorated sterling stopper.

S44 A cologne in a border and miter pattern with a silver stopper.

S46 A flask with a sterling silver stopper.

S47 A puff box with initials in center of decorated lid.

R48 A cigar jar with an ornated pattern and highly decorated combined lid and knob handle.

S49 A bowl with a silver rim.

C50 A jewel box with hinged rims and a stubby handle on upper one.

C51 A jewel box with hinged rims.

S52 A glove box with hinged rims and hobstar motif.

S53 A glove box with hinged rims and opened using clip at front.

S54 A handkerchief box with hinged rims.

C55 A tall jug with a silver spout.

C56 A decorated spout signed Gorham on the silver.

C57 A decorated silver rim on a vase.

R58 Heavily decorated silver rim and handles signed Gorham on a loving cup.

R59 Silver candle holders on a candelabra.

R60 Five silver candle holders on a candelabra.

C61 A 10-inch bowl in the Columbia pattern by Quaker City with combination minor connecting motifs.

C62 A nappy cut with pinwheels connected by combination minor motifs in Hoare pattern #1397.

C63 A handled comport with hobstars linked with combination minor motifs.

S64 A comport in #55 and signed by Libbey connects hobstars with combination minor motifs.

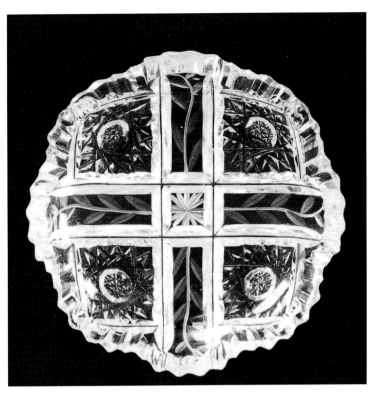

S65 A small bowl with bar outline.

S67 A vase cut in two hobstar borders and notched miters.

C66 Left carafe uses rows to outline the pattern and one on right favors hobstar dominant motif and combination minor motifs.

C68 A tray with outline of pattern created with stars that connect the large hobstars.

C70 A low bowl cut with alternating panels.

P69 A 10-inch vase outlines the pattern with gothic arches.

C71 A vase with swirled and alternating panels with border on the neck.

C73 Circles of small stars frame the dominant hobstars.

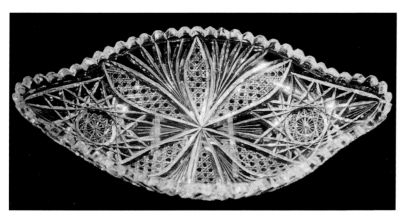

C72 A 14-inch tray that uses pointed loops to unite the hobstars.

C75 Panels join with loops unite the flashed single star.

C74 Panels and rows form the pattern on this jug.

C76 Panels and pointed loops form the pattern on this large bowl.

C77 Fans enhance the stars near the base.

C78 The major and minor motifs combine to form units.

C80 A combination of minor motifs unite the design on a square bowl.

C79 A tall vase repeats the units three times.

Chapter 5
Identifications of Patterns

Identification relies on locating a signature, matching a pattern, or both. Either can lead you to the company that produced the piece of cut glass.

A factory produced the piece from blank to completion of cutting. A cutting shop bought the blank and cut the design. Mostly we have based these identifications of patterns on company catalogs. You may have already identified one or more from another source.

T.B. Clark & Company
Cutting Shop
1. Geometric Patterns:
Vase in Cypress (**C81**)
Jug in Flemish Odel (**P82**)
Henry VIII claret jug with Reed and Barton on silver rim (**P83**)
Mistletoe in flower pot with capped diamond (**C84**) and vase (**C85**) with crosshatching.
2. Signed
Club-shaped nappy (**S86**)

C. Dorflinger & Sons
Factory
Numbered patterns included footed jug #99 (**C87**) tumbler 293 (**S88**).

H. C. Fry Glass Company
Factory
Geometric Patterns: two handled comport in Astoria (**C89**) whiskey jug in Japan and signed (**P90**), celery in Taxi (**C91**), #50334 (**S92**).

T. G. Hawkes & Company
Cutting Shop
1. Geometrics
10-inch bowl in Armanda (**S93**)
8-inch bowl in Astor (**S94**)
3 vases in Brunswick (**P95**)
Chrysanthmum (**C96**)
Columbus plate (**S97**)
Tumbler in Cut and Water Cress (**C98**)
Oils in Delft Diamond (**S99**)
Upright celery, English (**S100**)
Cologne in Holland (**S101**)
Bowl in Hudson (**C102**)
Nappy in Jupiter (**P103**)
Tray in Kohinoor (**C104**)
Bowl in Manlius (**S105**)
Carafe in Marion (**S106**)
Spoon tray in Mona (**S107**)
Match Holder in Navarre (**P108**)
Vase in Oriental (**P109**)
Jug in Prudence (**C110**)
9-inch bowl in Rex (**C111**) and signed
2. Numbered Patterns (Companies used a number rather than a name.)
Butter Pat #1 and #5 (**S112**)
Candlesticks #3010A (**S113**)
Relish #18267 (**S114**)
3. Signed
Square bowl (**P115**)
Triangular large bowl (**S116**)
Comport (**S117**)
Dish (**C118**)
Nappy (**S119**)
10-inch plate (**P120**)
Rose Globe (*C121*)
Toothpick holder on left (**S122**)
Tumbler (**S123**)
Tumbler (highball) (**S124**)
Tumbler (highball) (**S125**)
4. Gravic Glass (Floral designs Hawkes cut and signed.)
Plate in Aster (**S126**)
Cruet in Iris (**S127**)
Whiskey bottle in Thistle (**S128**)
7-inch plate in Tiger Flower (**S129**)
Hair receiver in Wild Rose and signed (**S130**)

J. Hoare & Company
Cutting Shop
1. Geometrics
Jug in McCedoz (**C131**)
Two jugs left to right, #575 (**C132**) and Melrose (**C133**)
Five inch vase in Melrose (**C134**)
12 x 12 punch bowl in Newport and signed (**P135**)
Nappy in Star and signed (**C136**)
2. Numbered Patterns
8 inch bowl #124 (**C137**)
Jug #631 (**C138**)
Nappy #1397 (**S139**)
Vase #1240 (**S140**)
Celery #1946 (**S141**)
3. Signed
11 inch bowl (**P142**)
Divided nappy (**C143**)

Libbey Glass Company
Factory

1. Geometrics
Rose Globe in Brilliant and signed (**S144**)
9 inch bowl in Iona (**C145**)
8 inch bowl in Ivenia and signed (**S146**)
Cruet in New Brilliant and signed (**C147**)
9 inch bowl in Panel Star and signed (**C148**)
9 inch plate in Poppies (**S149**)
2. Numbered Patterns
Covered bonbon #7 (**C150**) and signed

Small comport #55 (**S151**)
Cruet #174 (**S152**)
3. Signed
Triangular low bowl (**C153**)
9 inch bowl (**C154**)
Pair of tumblers (**S155**)
Whiskey tumbler (**C156**)

Every time that you view cut glass, you may want to test yourself and see if you recognize any of these identifications.

P82 A jug in Flemish Odel by Clark.

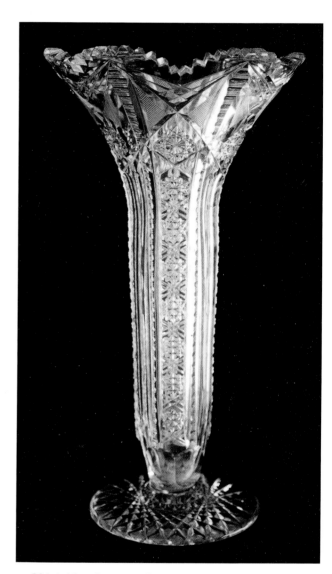

C81 A 16-inch vase in Cypress and signed by Clark.

P83 A jug in Henry Vill by Clark. The silver border signed Reed & Barton.

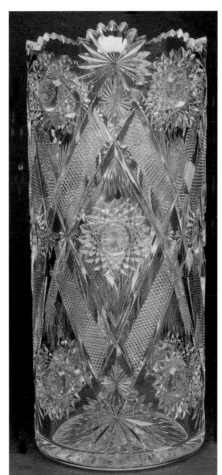

C85 A vase in mistletoe by Clark.

C84 A flower pot in Mistletoe by Clark.

S86 A club shaped bonbon signed Clark.

C87 A footed jug in Pattern #99 by Dorflinger.

S88 A tumbler in Pattern #293 by Dorflinger.

S89 A two-handled comport in Astoria by Fry.

S92 A vase registered #50334 and signed Fry.

P90 A whiskey jug in Japan Pattern by Fry.

C91 A celery tray in Taxi Pattern by Fry.

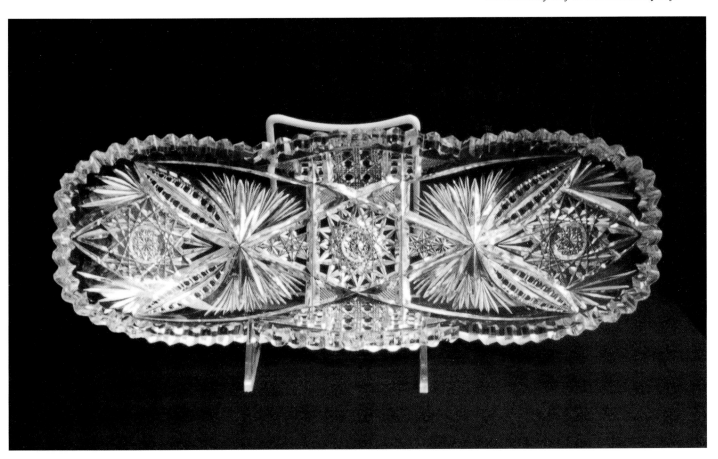

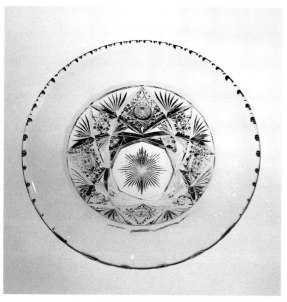

S93 A bowl in Armanda by Hawkes.

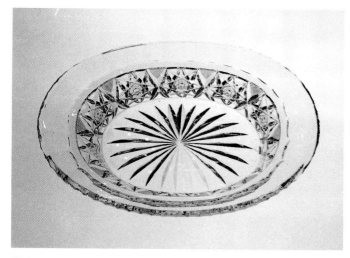

S94 A low bowl in Astor by Hawkes.

P95 Three vases (16", 12", and 10") in Brunswick by Hawkes and signed.

C96 An 11 1/2-inch vase in Chrysanthemum by Hawkes.

S97 Hawkes produced this small piece and named it Columbus.

S98 A water tumbler in Pattern Cut & Water Cress by Hawkes.

S99 A cruet set by Hawkes in Delft Diamond Pattern.

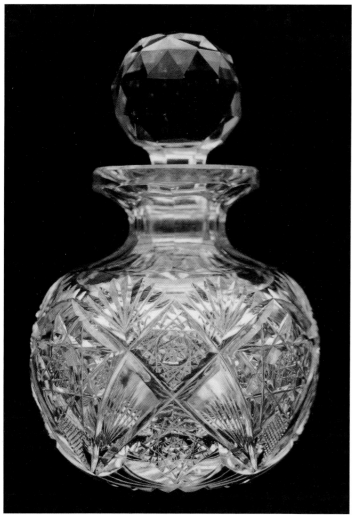

S100 Hawkes later called the Strawberry-Diamond pattern on this celery by the name of English.

S101 A cologne by Hawkes he called Holland.

C102 A bowl in Hudson Pattern and signed Hawkes.

P103 A nappy in Jupiter Pattern by Hawkes.

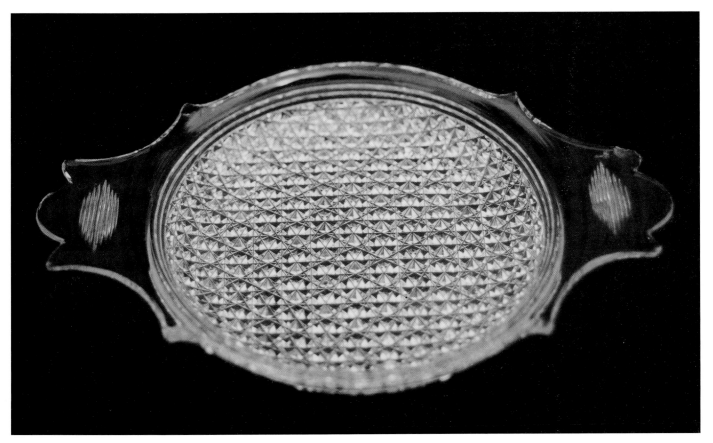

C104 An unusual tray in Kohinoor and signed Hawkes.

S105 A nappy in Manlius and signed Hawkes.

S106 A carafe in Marion Pattern by Hawkes.

S107 A spoon holder in Mona by Hawkes.

48

P108 A heavily cut match holder in Navarre and signed Hawkes.

C109 An 18-inch vase in Oriental Pattern by Hawkes.

C110 A jug in Prudence Pattern by Hawkes.

C111 A 9-inch bowl in Rex Pattern and signed Hawkes.

S113 A pair of 9-inch candlesticks signed Hawkes.

S112 Two butter pats (left to right) in #1 and #5 by Hawkes.

S114 An 11 1/2-inch celery, #18267, by Hawkes.

P115 An 8-inch square low bowl signed Hawkes.

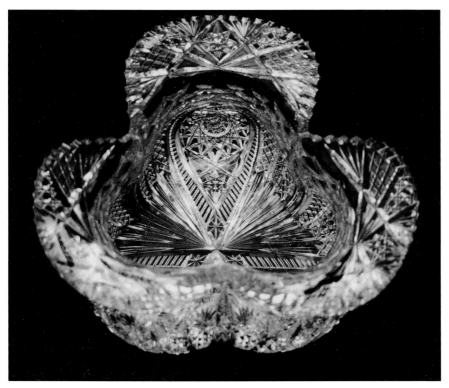

P116 A triple-shaped bowl by Hawkes.

51

S117 A 4-inch tall comport signed Hawkes.

C119 A handled nappy, 5 1/2-inches not counting the handle, signed Hawkes.

C118 A square shaped low bowl, 6 inches, signed Hawkes.

P120 A 10 3/4-inch plate signed Hawkes.

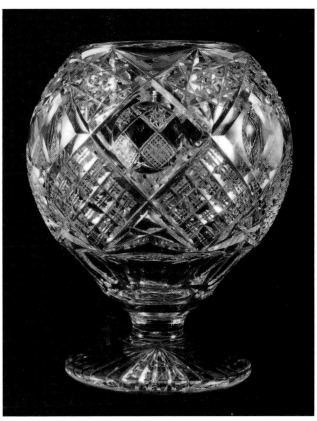

C121 A 7-inch tall rose globe signed Hawkes.

S122 Toothpick holder on left signed Hawkes.

S124 A highball tumbler signed Hawkes.

S123 A water tumbler signed Hawkes.

S125 Highball tumbler by Hawkes.

S126 A plate in Aster Pattern by Hawkes.

S128 A gravic cut whiskey bottle in Thistle Pattern by Hawkes.

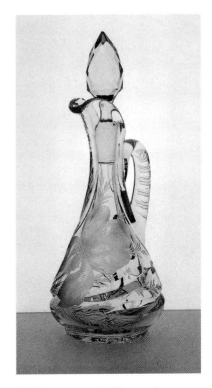

S127 A cruet in Iris Pattern by Hawkes called gravic glass.

S129 A 7-inch plate in gravic glass called "Tiger Flower" by Hawkes.

S130 A gravic cut hair receiver in Wild Rose Pattern by Hawkes.

S131 A jug in McCedoz Pattern by J. Hoare.

C132 & 133 Two jugs, one on right Melrose by Hoare and one on left unidentified.

P135 A 12-inch tall punch bowl in Newport Pattern by Hoare.

C136 A 4 1/2-inch piece signed Hoare in Star Pattern.

P134 A 17 1/2-inch tall vase in Melrose and signed by Hoare.

C137 Low bowl in numbered pattern #124 by Hoare.

C138 A jug numbered #631 by Hoare.

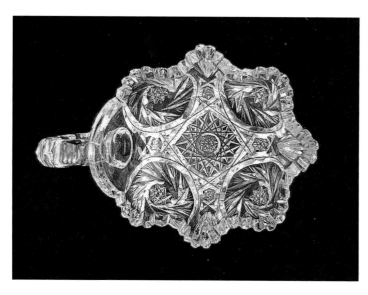

C139 A nappy in pattern #1397 by Hoare.

P142 A large bowl signed Hoare.

S140 A vase in pattern #1240.

S141 A 13-inch celery in pattern #1946
and signed by Hoare.

C143 A divided nappy signed Hoare.

S144 A rose globe signed Libbey in Brilliant Pattern.

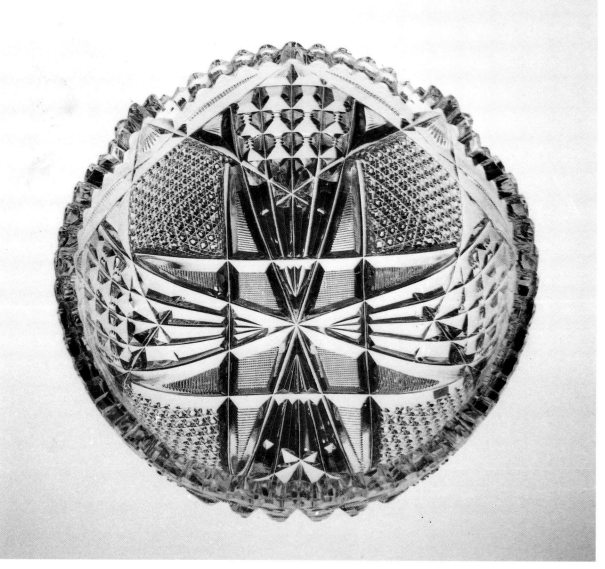

C145 A 9-inch bowl in Iona Pattern by Libbey.

C146 An 8-inch bowl in Ivenia by Libbey.

S147 A cruet in New Brilliant Pattern and signed Libbey.

C148 A 9-inch bowl in Panel Star by Libbey.

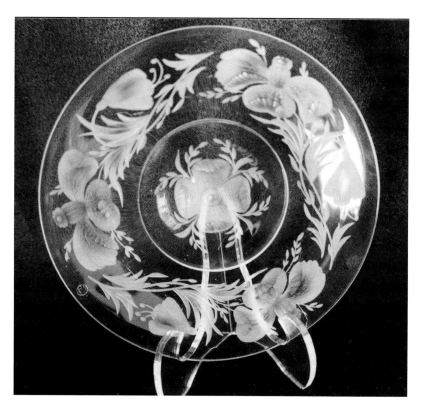

S149 A 9-inch plate in Poppies by Libbey.

C150 A 4 3/4-inch covered bonbon in #7 by Libbey.

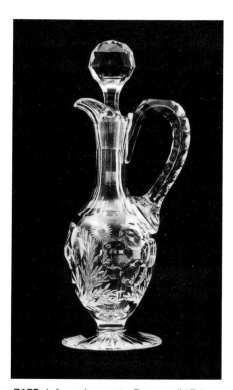

S152 A footed cruet in Pattern #174 by Libbey.

S151 A small comport in pattern #55 by Libbey.

C153 A triangular-shaped bowl signed Libbey.

S155 Two water tumblers signed with a Libbey sword.

C154 A 9-inch bowl by Libbey.

C156 A whiskey tumbler signed Libbey.

Chapter 6
Additional Pattern Identifications

Identifications of cut glass patterns never end. Both the large and small companies created new patterns they sold to jewelry stores, chain stores such as Sears-Roebuck. With the reprint of old catalogs, you have a constant opportunity to make new identifications of patterns. See if you have pieces with patterns that match any of these additional identifications.

C. G. Alford Jewelry Shop
Punch bowl 13-inches in Concord (C157)
Oil on right in Criterion (C158)
Carafe in Portland (S159)

Almy & Thomas
Cutting Shop
Signed 5-inch bowl (C160) and 9-inch low bowl (C161)

J. D. Bergen Company
Cutting Shop
Flower globe in Atlantic (C162)
Candlestick in Colonial (S163)
Mayonnaise bowl in De Soto (S164) and puff box (C165)
7-1/2-inch comport in Douglas (C166)
7-1/2-inch comport in Enterprise (S167)
8-inch bowl in Keystone (C168)
10-inch bowl in Renwick (C169)
Jug in Venus (C170)
Decanter in Winola (C171)
Toothpick holder (S172)

Blackmer Cut Glass Company
Cutting Shop
Punch bowl Radcliffe (P173)

Elmira Window Glasses Works
Cutting Shop
10-inch bowl in Enterprise (C174)
8-inch bowl #100 (C175)

Empire Cut Glass Company
Cutting Shop
Oil in Leader (S176)
Celery in Special (S177)
7-1/2-inch vase in Special (C178)

Gowans, Kents & Company Limited
Cutting Shop
A saucer (S179) signed

Gundy-Clapperton Company
Cutting Shop
17-inch vase with two handles (C180) and signed
3 footed dish and signed by company and Birks (S181)

Higgins & Seiter
Agent for Libbey and other companies
12-inch vase in Evertt pattern (S182)

G. W. Huntley
Wholesale
11-inch jug signed (S183) in India Pattern

Krantz-Smith & Company
Cutting Shop
Comport in Tokio (C184) and vase in Tokio (C185)

M A each circled with a C
Unknown
7 1/2-inch comport signed (S186)

Maple City Glass Company
Cutting Shop
Loving Cup in Cardinal (S187)

Marshall Field & Company
Department Store
Ice tub in pattern #74160 (C188)

Meridan Cut Glass Company
Cutting Shop
9-inch plate in Beverly (C189)
8-inch carafe in Byzantine (C190) and 10-inch bowl in same pattern (C191)
7-inch bowl in Shirley (S192), plate in Star Pattern (P193) wine jug in Strawberry-Diamond (S194) toothpick holder in #891 (S195)
Candelabra #8505 with Wilcox on the silver (P196)

Missouri Cut Glass Company
Cutting Shop
Cheese dome and matching underplate in Pears Pattern (C197)
8-inch bowl in Pennington Pattern (C198)

C. F. Monroe Company
Cutting Shop
Flower center in Norma (C199)

Mount Washington Glass Works
Factory
13-inch tray in Hexagon Diamond (C200)
13-inch tray unidentified (C201)

New England Glass Company
Cutting Shop
Rose globe in Middlesex (S202)

Ohio Cut Glass Company
Cutting Shop
Carafe in Fern (P203)

Oskamp, Nolting Company
Cutting Shop
Sherbet #9254 (**S204**)
Jug #9497 (**S205**)
Pairpoint Corporation
Silver and Cutting Shop
7-inch violet vase in Pansy (**S206**)
Persian with pinwheel (**S207**)
9-inch relish in Peru (**C208**)
7-inch ice tub in Willow (**C209**)
Comport in #81 (**S210**)
Punch ladle signed on silver (**P211**)
F. X. Parsche & Sons Company
Cutting Shop
9-inch bowl in Chrysanthemum (**C212**)
8-inch bowl in Crescent (**S213**)
Relish in Lotus (**C214**)
8-inch bowl in Primrose (**S215**)
Signed Celery (**C216**)
9-inch bowl (**C217**)
9-inch bowl (**C218**)
Pitkin & Brooks
Cutting Shop
14-inch tray in Zemona (**C219**)
Punch bowl in Zesta (**P220**)
Vase #634 (**C221**)
Signed Decanter (**P222**)
Quaker City Cut Glass Company
Cutting Shop
6-inch bowl in Champion (**S223**)
12-inch celery in Ellsmere (**S224**)
8-inch bowl in Pricilla (**C225**)
H. P. Sinclaire & Company
Cutting Shop
13-inch plate in Chrysanthemum (**S226**)
Match holder in #1 (**S227**)
#4 Jug (**C228**) and matching tumbler (**C229**)
#1021 and signed 9-inch bowl (**C230**)
Signed Candlestick (**S231**)

Clock (**C232**)
Comport (**S233**)
Sterling Cut Glass Company
Cutting Shop
Tall comport in Jupiter (**S234**)
L. Straus & Sons
Cutting Shop
Rose globe in Antoinette (**S235**)
Small jug in Columbus and signed (**C236**)
Carafe in "Drape" (**C237**)
5-inch finger bowl in Encore (**C238**)
8-inch bowl in Peerless (**C239**)
Jug and six tumblers in Venetian (**P240**)
Signed Flower center (**P241**)
17-1/3-inch tray (**P242**)
Taylor Brothers
Cutting Shop
11-inch tall jug in Leona (**C243**)
8-inch bowl in Waldorf (**C244**)
Signed 11-inch celery (**C245**)
Tuthill Glass Company
Cutting Shop
8-inch low bowl in Grapes (**S246**)
Small bowl in Phiox (**S247**)
Signed 10-inch celery (**C248**) Small comport (**S249**)
12-inch vase (**S250**)
Unger Brothers
Silver and Cut Glass
8-inch low bowl in Avondale (**S251**)
17-1/2-inch vase in Clairemont (**P252**)
9-inch bowl in Viola (**C253**)
Wilcox Silver Plate Company
11-inch jug #1449 with sterling rim (**S254**)
5-inch muffineer in Arlington (**S255**)
Sugar Sifter in Prism (**S256**) signed on silver
4-inch tumbler in Savoy (**C257**)

If you continue to buy American cut glass, you can easily learn about the glass produced by these companies.

P157 A 13 1/2-inch punch bowl in Concord Pattern by C. G. Alford.

C158 Oil on left in Criterion Pattern by C. G. Alford.

S159 Carafe in Portland Pattern by C. G. Alford.

C160 A 5-inch bonbon signed Almy & Thomas.

C161 A 9-inch bowl signed Almy & Thomas.

C162 Flower globe in Atlantic Pattern by Bergen.

S163 Candlestick in Colonial Pattern by Bergen.

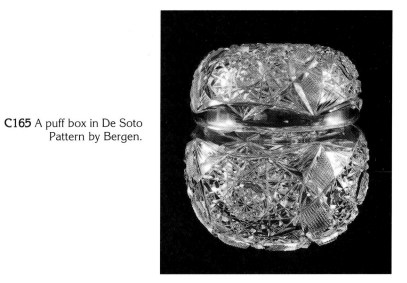

C165 A puff box in De Soto Pattern by Bergen.

S164 Mayonnaise bowl in De Soto Pattern by Bergen.

C166 A 7-inch tall comport in Douglas Pattern by Bergen.

S167 A 7 1/2-inch tall comport in Enterprise Pattern by Bergen.

C168 A bowl in Keystone Pattern by Bergen.

C169 A 10 1/2-inch bowl in Renwick Pattern by Bergen.

C170 A jug in Venus Pattern by Bergen.

C171 A decanter in Winola Pattern by Bergen.

S172 A toothpick holder
signed by Bergen.

P173 A punch bowl in Radcliffe Pattern by Blackmer.

C174 A 10-inch bowl in Enterprise Pattern with hobstar by Elmira.

C175 An 8-inch bowl in Pattern #100 by Elmira.

72

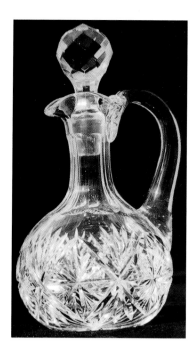

S176 An oil in Leader Pattern by Empire.

C178 A 7 1/2-inch vase also called "Special" by Empire.

S177 A celery called "Special" in Empire Catalog.

S179 A saucer signed by Gowans, Kent & Company.

S181 A 3-footed dish signed by Gundy-Clapperton Company and Birks.

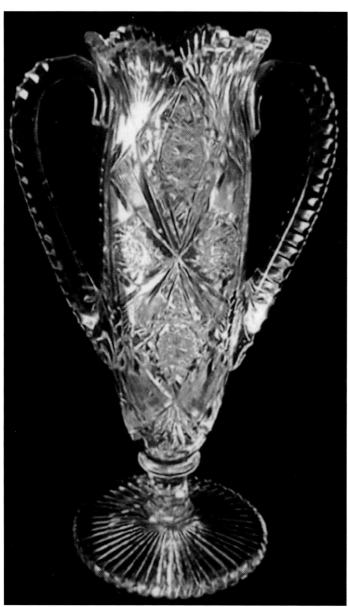

C180 A 17-inch vase signed by Gundy-Clapperton Company.

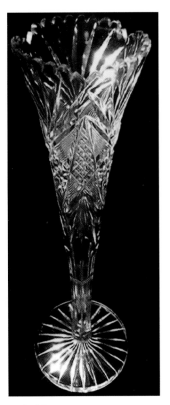

S182 A 12-inch vase in Everett Pattern by Higgins & Seiter.

C184 A 12-inch vase in Tokio by Krantz-Smith & Company.

C183 A 11-inch jug sold by G. W. Huntley, a wholesaler.

75

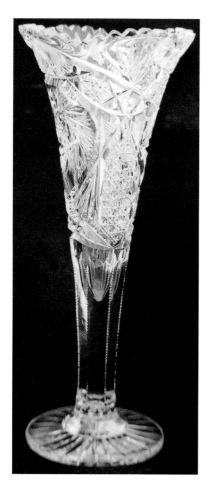

C185 A vase in Tokio by Krantz-Smith & Company.

S187 A loving cup in Cardinal by Maple City Glass Company.

S186 A 7-inch tall comport signed by M and A in a circle.

C188 An ice tub in #74160 by Marshall Field & Company.

C190 An 8-inch carafe in Byzantine Pattern by Meriden.

C189 A 9-inch plate in Beverly Pattern by Meriden.

C191 A 10-inch bowl in Byzantine Pattern by Meriden.

S192 A 7-inch bowl in Shirley Pattern by Meriden.

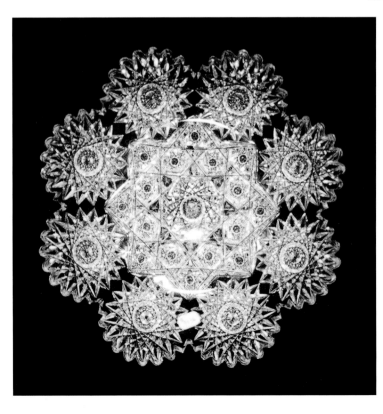

P193 A plate cut in the Star Pattern by Meriden.

S195 A toothpick holder in #891 Pattern by Meriden.

S194 A wine jug in Strawberry-Diamond Pattern by Meriden.

P196 A candelabra #8505 by Meriden with Wilcox on silver.

C197 A cheese dome and underplate in Pears Pattern by Missouri Glass Company.

C198 An 8-inch bowl in Pennington Pattern by Missouri Glass Company.

C199 A flower center in Norma Pattern by C. F. Monroe.

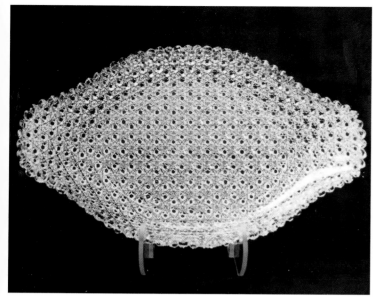

C200 A tray in Hexagon Diamond cut by Mount Washington.

S202 A rose bowl in Middlesex Pattern by New England Glass Company.

C201 A 13-inch tray cut by Mount Washington.

P203 A carafe cut in Fern Pattern by Ohio Cut Glass Company.

S205 A pattern numbered #9497 and cut by Oakamp, Nolting Company and signed.

S204 Two sherberts in pattern #9254 by Oakamp, Nolting Company.

S206 A 7-inch violet vase in Pansy Pattern by Pairpoint.

C209 A 7-inch ice tub in Willow Pattern by Pairpoint.

S207 A comport with a pinwheel in Persian by Pairpoint.

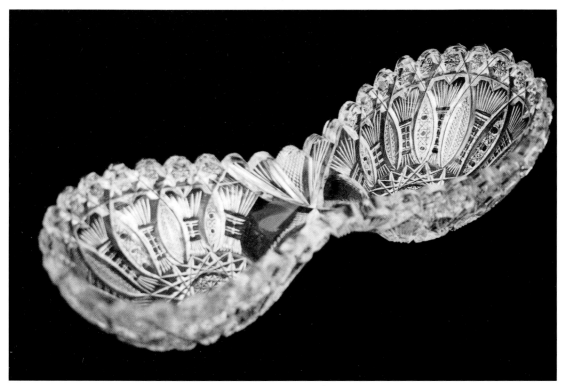

C208 A 9-inch relish dish in Peru Pattern by Pairpoint.

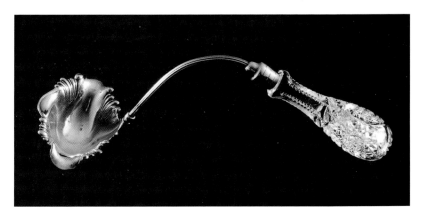

P211 A 13 1/2-inch punch ladle signed on silver by Pairpoint.

S210 A comport with silver rims on foot and edge numbered #81 by Pairpoint.

S213 An 8-inch bowl in Crescent Pattern by Parsche.

C212 A 9-inch bowl in Chrysanthemum Pattern by F. X. Parsche & Sons.

C214 A relish dish by Parsche in Lotus Pattern.

S215 An 8-inch bowl in Primrose Pattern by Parsche.

C217 A 9-inch low bowl signed by Parsche.

C216 A celery signed by Parsche.

P222 A signed decanter by Pitkin & Brooks.

C218 A 9-inch bowl signed by Parsche.

C219 A 14-inch tray in Zemona Pattern by Pitkin & Brooks.

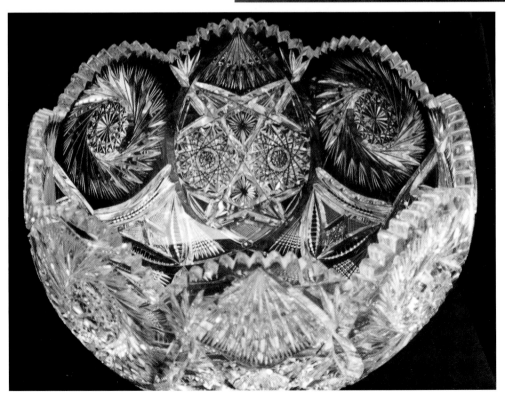

P220 A punch bowl in Zesta Pattern by Pitkin & Brooks.

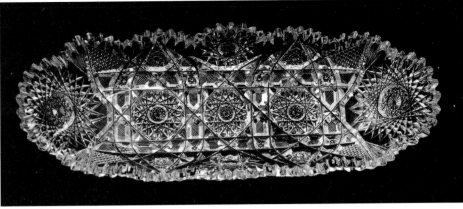

S224 A 12-inch celery in Ellsmere Pattern by Quaker City.

C221 A 12-inch vase numbered #634 by Pitkin & Brooks.

C225 An 8-inch bowl in Pricilla Pattern by Quaker City.

S223 A 6-inch bowl in Champion Pattern by Quaker City Cut Glass Company.

S226 A 13-inch plate in Chrysanthemum by Sinclaire & Company.

S227 A 2-inch high match holder numbered #1 and signed by Sinclaire.

C229 A tumbler that matches the jug in #4 pattern by Sinclaire.

C228 A jug, 8 inches high, in Pattern #4 by Sinclaire.

C230 A 9-inch bowl in Pattern #1021 by Sinclaire.

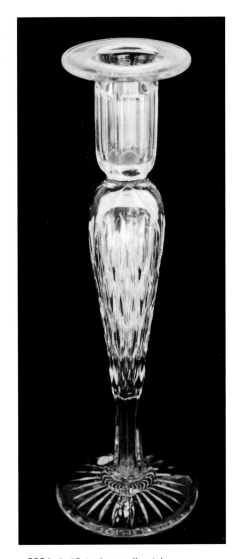

S231 A 12-inch candlestick signed Sinclaire.

C232 A clock signed Sinclaire.

S233 A comport signed Sinclaire.

S234 A comport in Jupiter Pattern by Sterling Cut Glass Company.

C236 An 8-inch tall jug in Columbus Pattern by Straus on a Libbey blank.

S235 A rose globe in Antoinette Pattern by L. Straus & Sons.

C237 A 7-inch carafe in a "Drape" pattern by Straus.

C238 A 5-inch finger bowl in Encore Pattern by Straus.

P241 A flower center signed by Straus.

C239 An 8-inch bowl in Peerless Pattern by Straus.

P240 A jug and six tumblers in Venetian Pattern by Straus.

91

P242 A 17 1/2-inch tray signed by Straus.

C244 An 8-inch bowl in Waldorf Pattern and signed by Taylor Brothers.

C243 An 11-inch tall jug in Leona Pattern by Taylor Brothers.

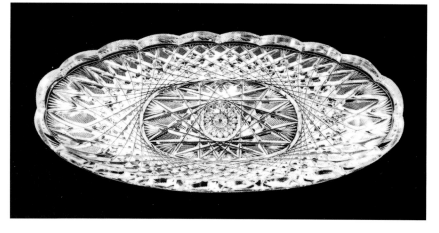

C245 An 11-inch celery signed by Taylor Brothers.

S246 An 8-inch low bowl in Grapes Pattern by Tuthill.

C248 A 10-inch celery signed by Tuthill.

S247 Small bowl in Phlox Pattern by Tuthill.

C249 A small comport signed Tuthill.

S250 A 12-inch vase signed Tuthill.

S251 An 8-inch bowl in Avondale Pattern by Unger Brothers.

P252 17-1/2-inch vase in Clairemont Pattern by Unger.

P253 A 9-inch bowl in Viola Pattern by Unger.

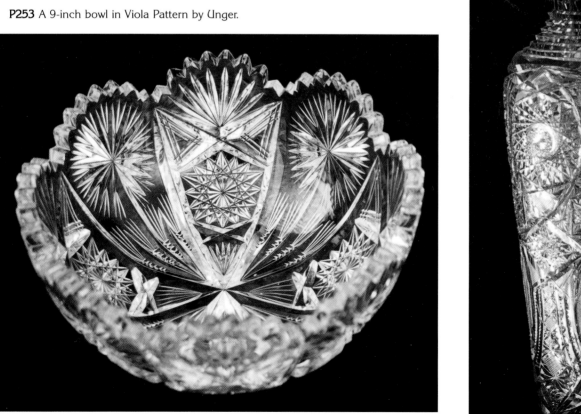

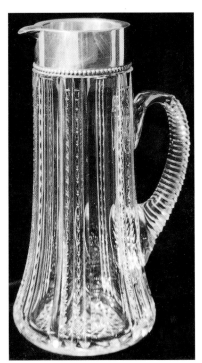

S254 An 11-inch jug with sterling rim in numbered Pattern #1449.

S255 Muffineer, 5 inches tall, in Arlington Pattern and signed Wilcox.

S256 Sugar sifter in Prism Pattern and signed Wilcox on silver.

C257 Tumbler in Savoy Pattern illustrated in Meriden-Wilcox Catalog.

Chapter 7
Colored Cut Glass

When you mention American Brilliant cut glass, some people quickly visualize a piece of heavy crystal, as a bowl, decanter, or nappy—all with ornate patterns. American companies also produced color-cut-to-clear glass in limited quantities during the Brilliant Period. Through the years this colored glass has greatly increased in value and becomes more desirable by buyers. The Americans created the finest colored cut glass. Before you rush to buy any colored glass, do get acquainted with the dominant features of both American and foreign production.

American Features

Specific facts about colored glass prove difficult to find. We interviewed knowledgeable people, such as dealers, retired craftsmen, members of families involved in the production for the following information.

1. Production Process The American companies overlaid the color on the crystal. The craftsman used two pots of metal; clear and colored. The pots contained the same temperature. To prepare for the overlay, the gatherer handed the blower a pipe with enough clear metal to create the desired piece. The blower shaped the metal slightly and returned it to the gatherer who spun it around in the colored metal until it reached the desired thickness. The pipe then went back to the blower who completed the shape. In this overlay process, you may see a division along the top edge between the clear blank and the color overlay.

2. Production Dates Most authorities agree that companies produced this colored glass in the 1880s following the Centennial Exposition and until the early 1900s when companies began to reduce costs. The fact that some American companies produced this colored glass in their popular patterns, such as Persian (**P258**) and Crosecut Diamond (**S259**), may suggest a possible date if the company applied for a patent. Yet no positive proof exists as to the date the company cut the pattern in color. So the dates of production prove vague.

3. Basic Colors Each company used its own private recipes and kept them secret from competitors. Even within companies the shades of color varied ever so slightly with the batch. American companies, however, favored a medium shade in green as on this bowl (**C260**), ruby in this jug (**C261**), cranberry in the Imperial Pattern by Straus (**S262**), and blue occasionally as

on this bell (**S263**). A rainbow color covers this decanter (**C264**). The shades varied slightly from batch to batch.

4. Production Companies The new colored glass appeared to increase sales, so two types of companies began to produce it. A factory blew the blank, cut the design, and sold it. The factories included such companies as Libbey, Mount Washington, Pairpoint, Dorflinger, and Fry. They sold blanks to cutting shops that included Clark, Hawkes, Hoare, Bergen, and others. Sometimes you can identify a company by matching the pattern in the company catalog. A Hawkes catalog does offer pieces cut in red or green.

5. The Blank Americans blew heavy blanks that contained considerable lead. The lead in the recipe gave the blank a special brilliance and extra weight.

6. Signature Very few companies signed the pieces of colored cut glass. We have seen a water carafe signed Clark, a sugar and cream with a Libbey signature.

7. The Patterns As you become familiar with patterns in American cut glass and the motifs used repeatedly, you can recognize American ones. A quick comparison to a foreign piece can help with this recognition.

Features of Foreign Glass

Foreign companies produced colored cut glass a number of years before the Americans. As the American took over the leadership in producing cut glass, foreign companies began to either copy or slightly change their glass.

1. Production Process The foreign companies leaned toward flashing the glass. The blower created the complete blank and then turned it over to the gatherer. This craftsman dipped the blank into the colored metal, the same temperature as the crystal one. Only a thin layer clung to the blank. This type of flashing would wear off with frequent use and washing (**S265**).

2. Production Dates Some references state that Egypt early began to cut glass but did not give the years. Certainly the Bohemian early began to produce cut glass (**S266**) as did other foreign countries. The published authorities fail to give extensive details.

3. Basic Colors Possibly the American companies used the same colors as the foreign companies. You can find signed pieces in blue (**S267**), by the Bohemians. The blue varied from light blue (**S268**) in a decanter to a blue green in a wine (**C269**) by St. Louis Glass Company to a dark blue (**C270**).

The red varied from ruby in a comport (**C271**) to a cranberry vase (**C272**). Val St. Lambert cut these wines in yellow (**S273**), green (**S274**), and cranberry (**S275**). On this vase in Bohemian glass the dark red looks almost black (**S276**). Foreign companies used solid colors as in this vase (**S276**) and these two colognes (**C277**) of cranberry and in (**C278**) in a bright blue. This cologne (**C279**) combined ruby with yellow. A European company probably produced the vase in green cut to clear (**S80**).

4. Production Companies and Signatures Stevens and Williams of England produced this plate (**S281**). Val St. Lambert copied this pattern from a Hoare one called Acme (**S282**). This company also signed this comport in crystal and blue (**S283**). The Bohemians produced a large amount of cut glass (**S284**). The St. Louis Company of mid-Europe also shipped cut glass to the United States.

5. The Blank These foreign and modern day companies rely on thin blanks. Because of less lead in the formula the pieces weighed less as in this hock wine (**C285**) and combined two colors.

6. Limited Recognition The lack of foreign company catalogs do restrict identification. A collector identified this piece as "made in Poland" (**S286**). Rather than name a specific foreign country, the collectors who furnished these photographs of pieces designated them as made in Europe: a container in green with squares and ovals (**S287**) and a vase with squares and flowers (**S288**). Pieces with an extensive use of fans indicated European production: (**S289**) and (**S290**).

Modern cut indicated a cranberry vase produced in Europe but only 5-1/2 inches tall (**S291**), and a vase in yellow with buzz (**S292**)and fan motifs (**S293**). Germany produced colored cut glass as with this comport containing clear ovals (**S294**) and this vase with a German bird cut in the design (**S295**). This ruby stein with a deer and a lid of aluminum (**S296**) suggests Germany.

This wine jug (**S297**) with aluminum neck and handle looks European. The blue punch bowl sold at an estate auction of a collector of American cut glass. The pre-list of pieces for sale gave no identification (**C298**) as American. The pattern on this whiskey jug we found on a number of different shapes (**C299**). The clear oval indicates European production. Any of the motifs of this pattern (**S300**) look foreign as does the design of this wine (**C301**).

At every opportunity carefully examine colored cut glass. You will learn very quickly to separate American glass from that produced by foreign companies. Oddly enough, looking for these special features will become almost instinctive. In this way you prepare yourself to buy American cut glass.

P258 An 8-inch fruit basket in ruby and Persian Pattern.

S259 A blue wine glass in Strawberry Diamond.

C261 A ruby colored jug with cross-hatching, fans, and hobstars.

C260 An 8-inch green bowl cut with hobstars, fans, and cane.

S262 A cranberry wine in the Imperial Pattern by Straus.

S263 A blue dinner bell, 7 inches tall, in Strawberry-Diamond and Fan.

C264 A rainbow of colors decorates this 14-inch decanter.

S265 A vase in a purple color cut by the Bohemians and signed.

S267 An 11-inch cobalt bowl produced in Europe.

S266 An 11-inch blue bowl produced by the Bohemians.

S268 A 14-inch light blue decanter made in Europe.

C269 A wine in light blue signed by St. Louis Glass Company.

C270 A blue 12-inch vase with clear ovals that suggests foreign origin.

P272 A cranberry vase with a pattern that looks European.

S271 A ruby jewelry box with silver rim looks foreign.

S273 A hock wine, 8 1/2-inches, signed Val St. Lambert.

102

S274 A hock wine in the same pattern but colored green and signed by Val St. Lambert.

S276 A 12-inch dark red vase in Bohemian glass.

S275 A cranberry wine produced and signed by Val St. Lambert.

C278 A blue cologne with a panel design that indicates foreign production.

C277 A solid colored cranberry cologne of foreign origin.

C279 The ruby and yellow colors suggest foreign production.

S280 The motifs and pattern of this green vase suggest foreign production.

S281 Steven and William in England created this plate.

S282 In this wine Val St. Lambert copied a Hoare pattern called Acme.

S283 Val St. Lambert produced this blue and crystal comport.

S284 This dark colored glass Bohemia created.

C285 This combination of yellow and ruby marks this as created in Europe.

S286 This vase in green and cut with fans the owner said came from Poland and possibly produced in modern times.

S287 The pattern with clear ovals and squares with odd star suggest European origin.

S288 The pattern, the color, and the shape point to European creation.

S289 A small wine in cranberry with fans dominating. The very light weight indicated foreign production.

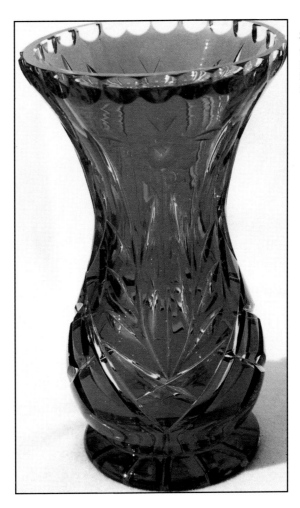

S291 A simple pattern on a cranberry vase resembles present-day patterns sold in department stores and individual shops.

S290 An 81/2-inch hock wine uses fans to border the other motifs.

S292 This yellow 8 1/2-inch vase uses the buzz and clear circles typical of present European glass.

S293 This dark yellow or brown vase with fan and buzz indicate an European piece cut fairly recently.

S295 A green vase with the bird native to Germany.

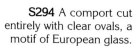

S294 A comport cut entirely with clear ovals, a motif of European glass.

S296 A ruby stein with aluminum lid, typically European.

S297 A ruby jug with handle and spout of aluminum, typical of European production.

C298 A blue punch bowl sold at the auction of an American cut glass collector, but list of pieces did not refer to it as American.

C299 A whiskey jug with a foreign pattern we found on a different shape.

C301 A pattern motifs suggest foreign creation.

S300 A comport in which pattern used European motifs.

Chapter 8
The Unidentified

When new collectors search for pieces of cut glass, they place beauty at the top of the list. They ignore company identification until they realize how much this fact can raise the value of a piece. As a result collectors have supplied us with pictures of unidentified pieces. But even experienced collectors, too, own the unidentified.

The American Cut Glass Association and various individuals have reprinted old catalogs found in attics, estates, and elsewhere for sale. Buy them. You may find an identification that will raise the value of a piece. To assist you in this identification we have listed the unidentified by shape, value, and pattern analysis.

The source of identification may include catalogs published by large or small companies, or those printed by wholesalers, agents, and shops. These independents may have purchased pieces from an individual who used a garage, barn, or back porch to produce the item. Sometimes you may find a name or number under the sketches in these last named catalogs.

When you buy a piece of brilliant cut glass, you may find an identification for one or more of these unidentified patterns. Do send the information to us at the publisher's address.

C302 A square bonbon bowl with a bar outline and major motifs of clustered hobstars.

S303 A 9-inch bowl with hobstar in square alternating with cane in squares.

C304 A 10-inch bowl with a combination panel and gothic arch outline and hobstars as dominant motifs.

P305 A footed bowl with decorated hobstar bars separating the large hobstars.

C306 10-inch candlesticks in border and miter outline but one with hobstar border and right with diamond one.

C307 A carafe with a star outline and hobstars as dominant motifs.

S308 A celery with a pointed loops outline and hobstars.

C309 A 12-inch celery with a border of 8 point stars and flashed single stars on the base.

C310 A bar outline with large hobstar motifs.

S311 A single star design on a small cologne.

C312 A pattern of hobstars and fans.

C313 A bar of stars separate the large hobstars.

C314 A flower center with 8-point hobstars bordered by fans.

C315 A flower center with a border of large hobstars directly above the base.

C316 A flower center with a triangle separating the large hobstar.

S317 A water jug with alternating panels of two hobstars and a combination of minor motifs framed in a diamond outline.

C318 A large jug with a bar of combination motifs between two overlapping hobstars.

C320 A tall jug with dual major motifs of buzzstar and flashed single star.

C319 A large heavy jug has hobstars separated by a unit of combination motifs.

S321 A large jug cut on a figured blank with only the flashed single star and butterfly cut.

C322 An ice bowl and matching underplate with 8-point star border and intaglio motifs.

C324 A handled ice bowl cut in a deep miter outline that frames the hobstars.

C323 Two-handled ice bowl with 8-point stars and fans.

S325 An ice tub with hobstars separated by x-bars of minor motifs.

C326 An ice tub with hobstars united with bars of cane.

P327 An ice tub with bars of single stars connecting the hobstars.

122

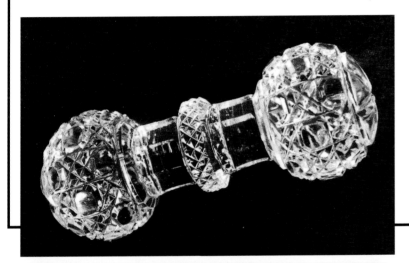

C328 Four knife rests cut in the standard shape with bars and knobs. Two have rings around the bar.

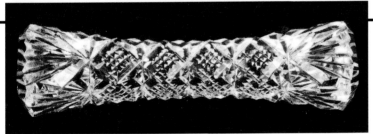

C329 A knife rest in a different shape cut in Strawberry-Diamond with a fan border.

C331 A lamp with a pointed dome and a major motif of a flashed single star.

S330 A lamp cut in Strawberry-Diamond and Fan.

C332 The dome of the lamp alternates stars in squares with connecting diamond shapes.

P335 Two lamps with pointed loops the same size that alternate between those with Strawberry-Diamond and those with a large hobstar.

C333 The dome circles hobstars that join with another rounded group in rows of stars.

C334 Dome with pointed loops outline does not match the base.

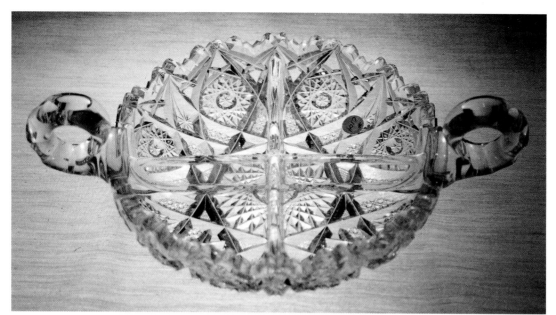

P336 A two-handled, divided nappy with hobstars.

C338 A punch bowl with a Gothic arch miter outline that encloses hobstars. Shapes has a turnover rim and low foot.

P337 A 12-inch plate that combines bars and circle outline with a hobstar in the circle.

P339 A punch bowl with a low foot joined to the large bowl by a ring with a row of crosshatching. A flashed simple star serves as the dominant motif linked by a unit of hobstars.

S340 The crossed bar outline unites the total cutting with Strawberry-Diamond motif.

S342 Bars frame the squares of strawberry-diamond cutting.

S341 A star outline uses minor motifs to accent the points.

S343 Two rose globes in different sizes with similar patterns using hobstars and fans.

S345 A toothpick holder with an engraved thistle.

S344 A small rose globe with an 8-point hobstar and fans.

S346 A toothpick holder with an attached tray.

S347 A pin tray with a center hobstar and border of double fans and stars.

S348 A band of 8-point stars framed by a diamond shape form a band around the tumbler.

C349 Parallel bars of two 8-point stars topped by a large fan form the panel outline united by a bar of small hobstars.

S350 Squares of crosshatching alternate with 8-point stars and fans to form the border for the parallel notched prisms.

S351 A whiskey tumbler with hobstars, a fan at the top, and parallel miters at the base.

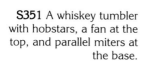

S352 A whiskey tumbler with flat hobstar as dominant motifs topped by fan. Later we found a Libbey signature.

S353 A circular vase cut in borders of hobstars and miters.

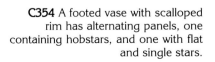

C354 A footed vase with scalloped rim has alternating panels, one containing hobstars, and one with flat and single stars.

C355 A footed vase with a cup shape at top uses hobstars as the dominant motif.

C356 In this vase hobstars dominate the cup, and stem contains, from bottom up, knob and flutes. A ring of flat star sits atop a square base.

P357 Hobstars dominate the pattern that sits on a base with a knob on the stem.

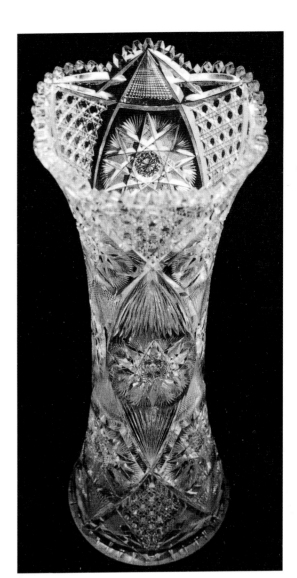

C359 A circular vase, smaller at the base than at the top has motifs of flashed stars, cane and fans.

C358 Hobstars and fans decorate this vase with a square foot and paneled neck.

C360 A vase in the border and miter outline using hobstars for the borders and notched prisms on the miters.

P362 A heavily cut vase with large flashed single stars framed top and bottom by row of hobstars.

P361 Two vases, left in bars and hobstars and right one cut in a different round shape with hobstars and flashed single stars.

Chapter 9
Buying Suggestions

Any flaw or damage on a piece of cut glass can affect the present and future value. So learn how to thoroughly examine the pieces for present condition before you buy them. Knowing about common flaws and where to find them will improve your buying ability.

Present Condition

Some flaws you can see easily, but with others you need to rely on touch. Knowing the type of flaw and where to look helps in finding it.

1. Chips A chip refers to a nick most often found on the top rim of various type pieces (**S363**) and on a base (**S364**). Sometimes you discover a chip along a deep miter of a large piece, such as bowls or comports. Feel the base dome edge of a covered butter or cheese. You can do this by feeling the areas without looking, but an experienced dealer will notice and credit your experience.

2. Flakes A flake or sliver refers to an elongated chip. A thin layer or sliver often gets knocked off the side of a rim or large miter. Do look or feel for a thinner width as the owner may have had it removed. To find a flake, use your forefinger and thumb to enclose the edge. Then run your finger along the miters, especially the deep ones and on the flat bottom of a stopper. The stopper may chip when put on a hard surface or returned to the neck.

3. Bruises A bruise consists of a cloudiness on the base or inside of open pieces caused by wear marks (small scratches) on a clear spot. You find bruises on the base of a tumbler or on heavy jars for tobacco, crackers, decanters, or jugs. These scratches a metal frog causes on any bowl used for a flower bouquet. Dealers refer to these scratches as wear or age marks as they indicate usage over a period of time. The sellers of new foreign glass sometimes place these scratches on pieces to pass them off as old according to one expert. You can have these wear marks removed if you think they mar the beauty of a piece, but some collectors prefer to leave them.

4. Fractures A group of small cracks form a fracture. The piece probably bumped against another or a hard surface. This damage occurs on the lips of jugs or decanters or on the rim of drinking ware. Dropping a stopper into the neck of a decanter can fracture it. A fracture defies repair, so do not buy any such damaged piece in spite of the low price.

5. Crush Points Unless you look closely, you will not see this tiny, white dot that represents a "crush point" on a piece of cut glass. A strong blow causes the crush point which can appear at any place on the piece. An attempt to remove it generally results in a crack or fracture. Unless the piece attracts your attention because of cheap price, don't buy it.

6. Cracks A crack indicates a break in the piece. You may or may not feel it. Generally, it follows a deep miter cut which makes it difficult to see. Holding the piece to a strong light sometimes makes the crack visible. You may try thumping the piece. Any piece that rings normally when thumped probably does not have a crack. A cracked piece may emit a flat tone. Check for other defects, such as a chip, to see if a crack developed from it. Cracks defy repair. Any who repairs glass constantly experiments with ways to repair cracked pieces.

7. Sick Glass A cloudy or frosted look may appear inside a vase or decanter. The acidity in vinegar, alcoholic beverages, salts, or perfume bottles can cause a chemical reaction that oxides the inner surface if left a long time in the container. Some people who repair cut glass may clear the inside temporarily by using a strong liquid or by grinding. This sickness appears only in shapes that contain the above liquids for a long time. To prevent sick cut glass empty the liquid after use and rinse thoroughly.

When you rinse a piece with water, the sick appears to disappear until it dries. Beware of a piece with water drops and don't accept the excuse that the owner recently washed it. You can temporarily remove the white by spraying the inside with cooking oil or nonstick spray.

Sometimes containers have an accumulation of residue, possibly from lack of thorough cleaning. Soak these pieces in a solution of false teeth cleaner. Never use a strong soap, such as that used in a dish washer. You may need to loosen the deposits with cotton on a swab stick. Since you never completely remove the deposits, hesitate to buy a piece with such residue.

Crazzle refers to another type of sick glass in which the crystals separate because of imperfect fusion of the metal or too short a time for annealing. Crazzle looks more like a web of minute fissures in the glass. An attempt to repair it makes the crazzle worse. Avoid buying any type of sick glass because repairs cost too much and to date permanent restoration proves impossible.

8. Heat Check In a heat check the top of the handle does not adhere to the blank. Since the worker placed the bottom of the handle first on the blank, the upper part sometimes cools too much for a perfect fusion. At other times the handle does not adhere to the blank. You can put your fingernail in the gap between the handle and the body of the piece.

When you place your finger over the outside handle, look inside the piece. You can see a white line where the handle did not fuse. Some believe that constantly holding the shape by the handle may force it to break off. We have not seen such a broken piece. No one has found a permanent remedy to adhere the handle. A heat check on the handle reduces the value.

Repaired Cut Glass

A dealer often says that damaged glass will not sell, so they must have it repaired. Repairs on cut glass divide into four categories.

1. Recut With a little practice you can recognize areas of recutting. A recut may remove the dip, too much of the clear space above the pattern or actually invade the pattern (**S365**).

The teeth on the edge of a rim originally showed a rounded shape as in this signed Libbey bowl (**C366**). Note these changes in the five recut rims (**S367**).

Do look for a match to an original cut that alternates the size of the scallops. In extreme repairs a recut may replace a scalloped rim with a straight one. Sometimes the cutter covered this straight rim with a plain silver band. Original silver bands usually contained a decoration and the trademark of the silver company.

To remove defects, the cutter may widen a large miter. This repair you may see or feel. The removal of a chip or sliver on the foot or base of an item may make it uneven. Place the piece on a hard surface and see if the removal makes in rock. A small repair of a base or a foot may remove the rounded edge and replace it with one slightly perpendicular. You can feel this change.

On a repair of an item with a spout, one side may measure thinner than the other, or the spout may have a snubbed look. Near the rim one side of a jug or a carafe may feel thinner than the other, indicating a recut. Always check for this difference in thickness.

2. Restore The restorer tries to return the flawed piece of glass to its original shape. This requires matching the thickness of the spout, the roundness of a foot, and the walls of a neck. Repairs may widen paralleled miters, level the base, and round the sawtooth edge. As a result you will need to truly search for good repairs (**C368**).

3. Restyle In repaired cut glass, think in terms of returning the piece to its original shape and function. In a number of cases, the person restoring the glass can not accomplish this. So the piece gets restyled (**S369**). At first glance the piece looks rare, but do keep looking. A

carafe becomes a rose bowl, or the bottom of a round vase gets made into a wine coaster. Parts from different pieces get put together (**S370**) and (**S371**).

4. Mending Broken Glass Glue used years ago to mend broken glass can turn yellow and dissolve. Recently, a talented repairman experimented with the glue doctors use in heart surgery. This colorless glue works so well you have trouble seeing the crack. Some bowls will even ring when thumped. To see the repair, you need to shine a strong light on it. If you feel sentimental about a broken piece, have it repaired with the water-proof glue.

Mate or Marriage

Mate means to put two matching pieces together. A marriage puts together two pieces with similar patterns and same function.

1. Underplate A number of shapes use an underplate. If you consider buying a dome covered cheese or butter, a mayonnaise bowl and plate, a sugar and cream, to name a few, carefully check the pattern for a match. Unmatched parts reduce the original value as with this jewel box (**S372**).

2. Stoppers and Lids Any time a decanter, cologne, or oil has a decorated stopper, very carefully check the pattern to see if it matches the one on the piece. After you check the pattern, note how the stopper fits into the neck. The wrong one will rock in the neck, not go into the neck area far enough, or go too far (**S373**). Don't buy a piece expecting to find a stopper unless you look for an ordinary one. Some dealers and those who restore cut glass do collect stoppers and lids, so you may find a match.

If a stopper gets broken, one from another ruined shape may be added (**S374**). Creative repairs may convert a different stopper (**S375**) or an amusing lid (**S376**).

With a silver lid you can only check the fit. Such pieces as cigar, cigarette, tobacco, or biscuit jars used flat silver lids. A hair receiver (**S377**) or a puff box gets married often. A knob added to the lid of a covered bonbon makes pattern matching more difficult.

3. Sugar and Cream Fortunately companies cut a number of similar shapes and patterns for a sugar and cream set. Breakage occurs frequently because of daily use. Don't get enticed with a rare and matching shape of any with a foot. Put the two side by side and truly compare the pattern. The checks, when used frequently, begin to stick in your memory, so rely on them.

Plus Values

When you buy a piece of brilliant cut glass, do look for an "extra" that will raise the value of a piece as time passes. Consider these suggestions that add a plus value to the item.

1. Inscription A number of pieces contain an inscription: personal gifts, a renewal of a subscription to a magazine, a souvenir for an organization at a national

name it! The inscription usually contains the date, the event, and any other needed information.

2. Additions Adding a foot, handles (**C379**), or a base gives the shape a plus value.

3. Original Liner The liner usually has the name of the company that produced it. Within recent years, silver plate or sterling liners someone has added to a fern. Some company in California lately has produced the silver lining, so don't pay the higher price for it as old original.

4. Inner Divisions The addition of clear divisions within a low bowl or nappy provides an upgrade in quality.

5. Signatures In recent years pieces have been signed with an electric needle. You can feel this signature. Furthermore these signatures do not always duplicate the original ones.

6. Large Shapes Instead of buying bowls and nappies, do look for larger shapes. Naturally they cost more, but they increase more in value. Look for a biscuit jar (**C380**), a tobacco jar (**C381**), a comport (**C382**), or pair of lamps (**P383**).

7. Odd Shapes A three part relish with a handle add an odd shape (**P384**). Epergnes you don't find without a concentrated hunt, but they increase rapidly in value: (**P385**), (**P386**), and (**P387**). This epergne (**P388**) actually rates a top evaluation.

8. Small Pieces Don't overlook well-cut and functional small pieces as this spoon tray by Parsche (**C389**), Worcestershire bottle (**C390**), or domed butter dish (**P391**), a dinner bell (**C392**), a clock (**C393**), or a Whimsey "shoe" cut as a miniature signed by Hoare (**C394**).

9. Sets Learn the pleasure in matching pieces to form a set. These two shapes in decanters and wine glasses began with the decanter and two clarets. The buyer found the handled decanter and now has twelve matching clarets (**P395**). You may want to match saucers to fruit bowls, butter pats, or knife rests.

Follow these suggestions when you shop for a piece of cut glass. The results will surprise you.

S363 A tumbler with a chip on the rim.

S364 The base of a vase with the chips removed.

C366 A bowl signed Libbey shows the rounded teeth of the rim.

S365 In removing chips from the rim the repairman cut into the pattern.

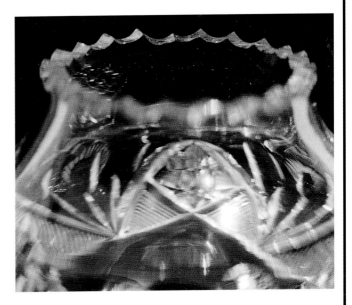

S367 Five recut rims that varied from the one used originally. The tall slender comport Pairpoint cut in pattern called Pansy.

C368 Two pictures show the jug and the restored one.

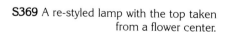
S369 A re-styled lamp with the top taken from a flower center.

S370 The foot does not match the pattern of the cup on this vase.

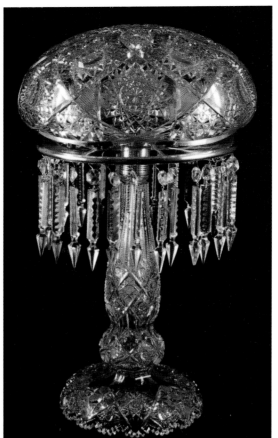

S371 The stopper gets married to the foot.

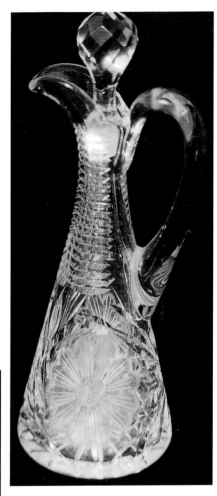

S373 The stopper does not go deep enough into the neck as the original would.

S372 The top does not match the bottom.

S374 The stopper added to the lid someone made a marriage.

141

S375 The stopper does not belong to the decanter.

S376 The repairman shows a sense of humor with this improvised lid.

S377 A marriage made between the bowl and the lid of this hair receiver.

C378 A square souvenir given at a national convention of the Masonic Lodge.

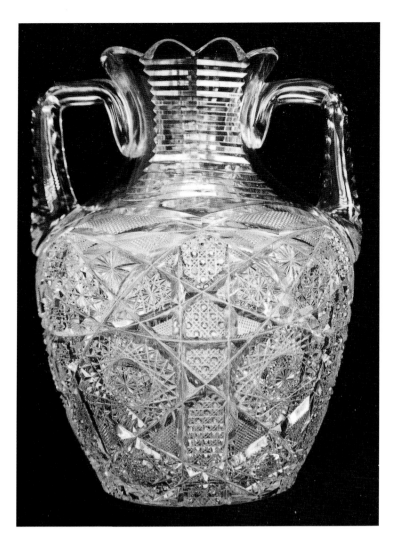

C379 The additional handles make this vase more valuable.

C380 A large piece in a biscuit jar will increase in value during the passage of time.

143

C381 A tobacco jar proves worthy of any extra search.

C382 A large comport that will increase in value.

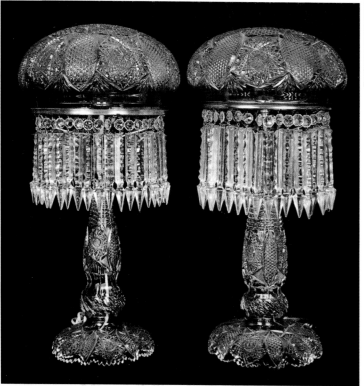

P383 A pair of matching lamps requires much search.

P384 A rare shape of a circular bonbon with a handle and design of flashed hobstars.

P386 An epergne heavily cut attracts everyone's attention.

P385 An epergne increases the value of any collection.

P387 Make sure that all parts of an epergne match as in this one.

C389 A spoon tray in a circular shape cut by Parsche.

P388 An epergne probably cut on special order.

P391 A heavily cut domed butter with matching underplate.

C390 A worchestershire bottle.

C392 A dinner bell found in limited numbers.

C393 A clock cut in a row outline.

147

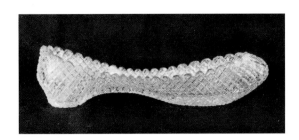

C394 A small shoe cut in Strawberry Diamond Pattern by Hoare.

P395 A set matched piece by piece.

Chapter 10
American Cut Glass Association

On July 29, 1978, a group of collectors and dealers met in Indianapolis, Indiana, to organize the American Cut Glass Association. One of our speaking engagements conflicted with the date, so we could not attend. We joined the Association a week later as a life member. In November of 1978, the Association incorporated in Texas.

The two groups wanted to learn more about American cut glass, the finest ever produced. In addition, collectors and dealers needed to get acquainted with each other. So those attending went to work on the constitution and by-laws (**396**).

Membership

Anyone interested in American cut glass and paid the dues could join the Association that offered three types of memberships.

1. Annual This person wanted to learn more about American cut glass and paid the annual dues to receive membership.

2. Life The prospective member could join for life and prepay the lump sum of dues. In the fall of 1999, the Association discontinued this membership.

3. Honorary Any person who did outstanding work for the Association may receive election of honorary status.

Officers

1. Board of Directors The Association divided the United States into four districts, Eastern, Southern, Central, and Western. The members elected two officers from each district and two at large. The two at large members must consist of a dealer and a collector. These elected members composed the board of directors, elected for one year. The president will serve as an ex-officio member of the board.

2. President Elected for one year, the president will preside at all meetings and serve as an ex-officio member of the board of directors. He will work with other officers and members of the board of director in arranging organizational meeting dates and locations.

3. Vice-President The Vice-President shall assume and perform the duties of the president when necessary.

4. Corresponding Secretary The corresponding secretary shall prepare and distribute the newsletter, *The Hobstar*. The membership made the editor of *The Hobstar* later a paid employee. At the same time the

membership established the paid executive secretary.

5. Treasurer This officer takes care of all money matters involving the Association and maintains a permanent record of the money.

6. Executive Committee This committee has the power to exercise the policies of the Board of Directors in the management of the Association during the interim between meetings of the board. Members include the President, elected Vice-President, and the immediate Past President.

Election Procedures

The President shall appoint a committee for the purpose of selecting a single slate of candidates to fill the elected offices of the Association. The nominating committee shall include one member from each of the four districts. The recommendation of the nominating committee shall go to the Board for approval. Voting of the membership may take place by mail. The Board will canvass all ballots.

Public Meetings

The Association will hold two types of meetings for the members.

1. National The Association will meet in July for a national meeting open to all. Members attending will have an opportunity to get acquainted with others.

The program at the National Convention includes speakers recognized for research in special fields of cut glass. In addition to dealer show offered opportunities to buy cut glass.

At first collectors displayed cut glass for show or sell in their rooms. The convention changed this to a scheduled evening where collectors could rent a space to sell, trade, or display cut glass. The members, whether dealer or collector, became acquainted when they shared meals.

2. Chapter Meetings Local members of the Association could request a charter giving permission to organize a Chapter. The meetings of the chapters depended on the organizers. Most met four to five times a year at restaurants or in the private homes to view private collections. Any chapter member must first join the Cut Glass Association.

3. Brilliant Weekend One or more local chapters may arrange for a Brilliant Weekend in the time span between the National Conventions. Usually the group met at an airport or nearby. They used speakers and a dealer show similar to the program of the National Convention.

4. Displays and Lectures Local chapters often set up a display at a public library, college, or public place and engaged speakers to discuss cut glass. Texas Agricultural and Mechanical College in Texas has continued the display it introduced adding other items.

The Hobstar

The connecting link between the members consisted of the publication of *The Hobstar*, now sent to members ten times a year.

1. Advertisements Various dealers advertise cut glass they have for sale, showing pictures of the pieces and providing accurate information.

2. Auctions *The Hobstar* publishes summaries of auctions prices so the collector can get an idea of value.

3. Identification *The Hobstar* has a knowledgeable committee that assists in identifying patterns and sources of production. If they do not know, they will print the picture of the piece in *The Hobstar* and invite others to help with identification.

4. Matching Service If you want to complete a set, send a picture to *The Hobstar* and ask for assistance.

5. Features *The Hobstar* publishes special features on cut glass, companies, and outstanding individuals in cut glass.

6. Catalog Reprints One project of *The Hobstar* includes the reprinting of old cut glass catalogs and offer-

ing them for sale. The Association now has 23 available for sale.

Financial Security

The American Cut Glass Association early established financial security from a number of different sources.

1. Memberships These dues went into the treasury. In the fall of 1999, as previously mentioned, The Association no longer needed life memberships to reinforce the treasury.

2. Reprint of Catalogs The reprinting and sale of old catalogs contributes extensively to the cost of operations. The Association now has 23 for sale.

3. Advertising in *The Hobstar* Antique dealers' advertising contributes to the treasury.

4. Dealer Show Space rent at the National Convention With more dealers joining the show at the National Convention, the amount of rent for space has increased.

5. Attendance Fees Fees for attending the dealer's show at the National Convention when opened to the public on Saturday afternoon.

The American Cut Glass Association grows yearly. It offers you a new interest in life and an opportunity to meet fascinating collectors and dealers. Cut glass can beautify the decor of your home. Most important, the Americans produced the finest cut glass in the world. So start today collecting American Brilliant Cut Glass and provide your life with an exciting new focus.

S396 Pictured are those who organized the American Cut Glass Association, with names listed by position.

Bibliography

Books

The Acorn, Journal of Sandwich Glass Museum, Vol. 8, 1995, 1998.

The American Cut Glass Industry, Antique Collectors' Club, Ltd., 1996.

Avila, George C., *The Pairpoint Glass Story*, New Bedford, Massachusetts: Reynolds DeWalt Printing, Inc., 1968.

Barlow, Raymond E. & Joan E. Kaiser, *A Guide to Sandwich Glass*, Atglen, Pennsylvania: Schiffer Publishing Ltd., 1987.

Boggess, Bill and Louise. *American Brilliant Cut Glass*. New York: Crown Publishers, Inc., 1977.

_____. *Collecting American Brilliant Cut Glass*. Atglen, Pennsylvania: Schiffer Publishing Ltd., 1992.

_____. Identifying American Brilliant Cut Glass. New York: Crown Publishers, Inc., 1984.

_____. Identifying American Brilliant Cut Glass. Atglen, Pennsylvania: Schiffer Publishing Ltd., 1991. Revised and enlarged edition with value guide.

_____. Boggess, Bill & Louise. *Reflections on American Brilliant Cut Glass*, Atglen, Pennsylvainia: Schiffer Publishing Ltd. 1995.

Collectors Illustrated Price Guide to Cut Glass. Paducah, Kentucky: Collectors Books, 1977.

Daniel, Dorothy, *Cut and Engraved Glass*. New York: M. Barrows & Company, Inc., 1950.

_____. *Price Guide to American Cut Glass*. New York: William Morrow & Company, Inc., 1967.

DiBartolomeo, Robert E. *American Glass*. Princeton, New Jersey: Pyne Press, 1974.

Ehrhardt, Alpha. *Cut Glass Price Guide*. Kansas City: Heart of America Press, 1973 (contains 8 catalogs).

Evers, Jo. *The Standard Cut Glass Value Guide*. Paducah, Kentucky: Collectors Books, 1975 (contains 5 catalogs).

Farrar, Estelle Sinclaire. *H. P. Sinclaire, Jr. Glass Maker v.1.* Garden City, New York: Farrar Books, 1974 (contains inventory photographs).

Farrar, Estelle Sinclaire and Jane Spillman. *The Complete Cut and Engraved Glass of Corning*. New York: Crown Publishers, Inc., 1979 (contains inventory pictures of Sinclaire glass).

Fauster, Carl U. *Libbey Glass*. Toledo, Ohio: Len Beach Press, 1979.

Feller, John Quentin. *Dorflinger America's Finest Glass, 1852-1921*. Marieta, Ohio: Antique Publications, 1988.

Fry Glass Club. *Encyclopedia of Fry Glass*. Paducah, Kentucky: Collectors Books, 1989.

Gillander, William. *Treatise on Art of Glassmaking*. 1954. Second Edition.

Glass Container Manufacturers Institute, *Billion of Bottles*. New York, 1959.

Historical Society of Middleton, Sixth Annual. 1958.

Hodkin, F. W. and A. Cousen. *A Text Book of Glass Technology*. New York. D. Van Nostrand Company, 1925.

Hotchkiss, John F. *Cut Glass Handbook and Price Guide*. Des Moines, Iowa: Wallace-Homestead Book Company, 1970.

Kovel, Ralph M. and Terry H. *A Directory of American Silver, Pewter and Silver Plate*. New York: Crown Publishers, Inc., 1901.

Libbey Glass, 1919-1968. Toledo, OH: Toledo Museum of Art, 1968.

Lightner Museum. *American Brilliant Cut Glass, Masterpieces from Lightner Museum*. St. Augustine, Florida. 1991.

McKearin, Helen and George S. *American Glass*. New York: Crown Publishers, Inc. 1946.

Mebane, John. *Collecting Bride Baskets*. Des Moines, IA: Wallace-Homestead Book Company, 1976.

Newman, Harold. *An Illustrated Dictionary of Glass*. London: Thames Publishing Company, 1977.

Oliver, Elizabeth. *American Antique Glass*. New York: Golden Press, 1977.

Padgett, Leonard. *Pairpoint Glass*. Des Moines, Iowa: Wallace-Homestead Book Company, 1979.

Pearson, J. Michael. *Encyclopedia of American Cut and Engraved Glass*. 3 volumes. Miami Beach, Florida, 1975-1977.

_____. *Adventures and Mis-Adventures of Antique Dealers and Collectors*, 1993.

Pearson, J. Michael and Dorothy T. *American Cut Glass for Discriminating Collectors*. New York, 1965.

_____. *American Cut Glass Collections*. Miami Beach, Florida, 1969.

Pennsylvania Glassware, 1870-1904. Princeton: The Pryne Press, 1972.

Phillips, David Brandon. *Objects of American Brilliant Period Cut and Engraved Glass, 1880-1910*. 1985.

Rainwater, Dorothy T. *Encyclopedia of American Silver Manufacturers*. Atglen, Pennsylvainia: Schiffer Publishing Ltd., 1986.

Revi, Albert Christian. *American Cut and Engraved Glass*. New York: Thomas Nelson & Sons, 1965.

_____. *The Spinning Wheel's Complete Book of Antiques*.

Schroeder, Bill. *Cut Glass.* Paducah, Kentucky: Collectors Books, 1977.

Spillman, Jane Shadel. *Glass Tableware and Vases.* New York: Alfred A. Knopf, Inc. 1982.

_____. *White House Glassware.* The White House Historical Association, 1989.

Stevens, George. *Canadian Glass, 1825-1925.* Toronto: Ryerson Press, 1967.

Swan, Martha Louise. *American Cut and Engraved Glass of the Brilliant Period.* Lonbard, Illinois: Wallace-Homestead Book Company, 1986.

The Story of California Cut Glass. Brock & Company, Los Angeles.

Victoria and Albert Museum. *Glass Table-Ware.* 1947.

Waher, Bettye W. *The Hawkes Hunter, 1880-1962.* 1984.

Warman, Edwin G. *American Cut Glass.* Uniontown, Pennsylvania: E. G. Warman Publishing, Inc., 1954.

Weiner, Herbert and Freda Lipkowitz. *Rarities in American Cut Glass.* Houston, Texas: Collectors House of Books Publishing Company, 1975.

Wilson, Kenneth M. *Glass in New England.* Old Stourbridge Meriden, Connecticut. 1969.

Catalogs

Alford Cut Glass, 1903, 1904.

Ben Allen & Company, 1924.

American Cut Glass Association Reprints:
> *Dorflinger: Line Drawings*
> *T.G. Hawkes & Company*
> *J. Hoare & Company catalog*
> *Maple City Glass Company and T.B. Clark & Company*
> *Meriden Cut Glass Company-Wilcox Silver Plate Company*

Averheck Rich Cut Glass: catalog #104, undated.

Baracat Catalogue.

Bergen Cut Glass Company: 1904-1905, 1907-1908.

Blackmer Cut Glass: 1904, 1906-1907.

Buffalo Cut Glass Company catalog.

T.B. Clark & Company: 1896, 1901, undated, 1905, 1908, undated.

Covington Cut Glass Company, 1915.

Cut Glass Illustrated American Brilliant Period, Henry Brenner, glass engraver.

C. Dorflinger & Sons: catalog #51, 1881-1921, undated.

_____: catalog Kalana Art Glass.

O.F. Egginton Company catalog.

Elmira Cut Glass Company catalog.

Empire Cut Glass Company, 1906, 1910, 1912.

H.C. Fry Glass Company catalog.

Fort Dearborn Watch & Clock Co. 1909.

Gundy-Clapperton Company, 1909, 1915.

T.G. Hawkes & Company: American Cut Glass Association catalog, 14 catalogs of Brilliant Period, two late catalogs, and advertising booklet, undated.

Higgins & Seiter: 1893, 1899, #7, #17, #19.

J. Hoare & Company: three catalogs with no dates, 1911 catalog, and undated scrapbook.

G.W. Huntley, 1913.

Irving Cut Glass Company, Inc. catalog.

Keystone Cut Glass Company catalog.

Kranz Smith & Co., Inc. 1900, 1904, 1908, 1911, 1912.

Lackawanna Cut Glass Company, two catalogs.

Laurel Cut Glass Company; two catalogs, one 1907, other undated.

Libbey Glass Company: 1893, 1896, 1898, 1904, 1905, 1908, 1909, 1900-1910, c. 1920, 2 undated.

Liberty Cut Glass Works catalog.

Linford Cut Glass Company catalog.

Lotus Cut Glass Company: No. 49, No. 50.

Luzerne Cut Glass Company: two catalogs with no dates.

Maple City Glass Company: 1904 #3, 1906, #5, 1991 #10.

Marshall Field, 1896.

Meriden Cut Glass Company catalog.

C.F. Monroe Company catalog #6, other undated.

Mt. Washington Glass Works: 5 catalogs of Brilliant Period.

Niagara Cut Glass Company: two catalogs.

Ottawa Cut Glass Company, 1913.

Pairpoint Corporation: American Cut Glass Association catalog and 5 undated catalogs.

Pairpoint Manufacturing Company Gold and Silver Plate, 1894.

Parcel Post Cut Glass Company catalog.

F.X. Parsche & Sons Company catalog.

Phillips Cut Glass Company catalog.

Phoenix Glass Company: 1893 and one undated.

Pitkin & Brooks: 1907 and 3 undated.

Powelton Cut Glass Company catalog.

Quaker City Cut Glass Company: two catalogs undated.

Rochester Cut Glass Company catalog.

Roden Brothers, 1917.

Silver Plate and Sterling Silver Catalogue of 1888 by W.G. Crook.

Sinclaire Sketches and Office Corresponces Papers.

Steuben Glass Works catalog.

L. Straus & Sons, 1893.

Taylor Brothers: two catalogs.

F.B. Tinker, 2 undated catalogs.

Tuthill Cut Glass Company, The Connoisseur.

Unger Brothers: two catalogs, 1906 and one undated.

Unidentified Salesman's Catalogue, 1890-1905.

Unidentified catalog, possibly Hoare.

Val Saint-Lambert, 1906, 1908.

Wallenstein Mayer Company, 1913.

Waterford Glass Company, undated.

Whitall, Tatum & Co. 1880.

Wilcox Silver Plate Company, undated.

Appendix
Signatures and Marks

SIGNATURES ON AMERICAN RICH CUT GLASS

C. G. ALFORD & COMPANY
New York, New York

J. D. BERGEN COMPANY
Meriden, Connecticut

ALMY & THOMAS
Corning, New York

T. B. CLARK & COMPANY
Honesdale, Pennsylvania

M. J. AVERBECK MANUFACTURER
New York, New York

C. DORFLINGER & SONS
White Mills, Pennsylvania

O. F. EGGINTON COMPANY
Corning, New York

IRVING CUT GLASS COMPANY
Honesdale, Pennsylvania

PAIRPOINT CORPORATION
New Bedford, Massachusetts

H. C. FRY GLASS COMPANY
Rochester, Pennsylvania

LACKAWANNA CUT GLASS COMPANY
Scranton, Pennsylvania

P. X. PARSCHE & SON COMPANY
Chicago, Illinois

T. G. HAWKES & COMPANY
Corning, New York

LAUREL CUT GLASS COMPANY
Jermyn, Pennsylvania

PITKIN & BROOKS
Chicago, Illinois

J. HOARE & COMPANY
Corning, New York

LIBBEY GLASS COMPANY
Toledo, Ohio

SIGNET GLASS COMPANY
Address unknown

HOBBS GLASS COMPANY
Wheeling, West Virginia

LYONS CUT GLASS COMPANY
Lyons, New York

H. P. SINCLAIRE & COMPANY
Corning, New York

HOPE GLASS WORKS
Providence, Rhode Island

MAJESTIC CUT GLASS COMPANY
Elmira, New York

STERLING GLASS COMPANY
Cincinnati, Ohio

HUNT GLASS COMPANY
Corning, New York

MAPLE CITY GLASS COMPANY
Hawley, Pennsylvania

IORIO GLASS SHOP
Flemington, New Jersey

NEWARK CUT GLASS COMPANY
Newark, New Jersey

TAYLOR BROTHERS
Philadelphia, Pennsylvania

TUTHILL CUT GLASS COMPANY
Middletown, New York

THE VAN HEUSEN CHARLES COMPANY
Albany, New York

UNGER BROTHERS
Newark, New Jersey

WRIGHT RICH CUT GLASS COMPANY
Anderson, Indiana

NATIONAL ASSOCIATION
OF CUT GLASS MANUFACTURERS

UNIDENTIFIED SIGNATURES

ASH BROS.

OM^EG^A

ELLIS

155

CANADIAN CUT GLASS SIGNATURES

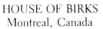

HOUSE OF BIRKS
Montreal, Canada

GOWANS, KENT & COMPANY LIMITED
Toronto, Canada

GUNDY, CLAPPERTON COMPANY
Toronto, Canada

PORTE & MARKLE

RODEN BROTHERS

Value Guide

The numbered illustration captions include letters that identify the *quality* of pieces in the photographs as follows:

S for Standard- **Standard** consists of a clear blank, simple pattern, and an ordinary shape.

C for Choice - **Choice** contains an ornate pattern, and an ordinary shape. Choice contains an ornate pattern, possibly a variance in shape, and an addition of a foot, handle or stopper.

P for Premium - **Premium** has an unusual shape and a very ornate pattern that entirely covers the blank.

R for rare - **Rare** refers to special order or a museum-type piece. Knowing the characteristics of American cut glass will help you recognize a rare American piece from that produced by foreign companies.

	Standard	Choice	Premium
BASKETS			
Bonbon	$150-300	$300-450	$460-600
Medium 12"	$250-400	$500-700	$750-2000
Flower 16"	$600-850	$1500-2500	$2000-3200
BELL			
Small 4"-5"	$125-175	$250-500	$500-850
Large 6"-7"	$200-300	$300-600	$600-1200
BONBON			
Handled 5"	$60-100	$100-200	$200-300
Covered 6"	$150-200	$200-300	$300-475
Footed 5"-6"	$200-250	$250-350	$350-550
BOTTLES			
Bitters w/top	$150-225	$250-400	$400-600
Cologne 6"	$300-375	$400-500	$500-1000
Ketchup	$125-200	$250-350	$350-500
Perfume 5"-6"	$200-275	$275-400	$400-675
BOWLS			
Finger	$75-100	$150-300	$325-450
Berry 8"	$150-225	$350-850	$1000-3500
Low 10"	$200-275	$350-850	$900-3500
Divided 9"	$175-300	$350-500	$600-1200
Handled/Footed	$175-300	$350-500	$600-1200
Orange 10"	$175-225	$250-400	$450-1250
Whipped Cream 6"-7"	$125-225	$250-400	$425-700
BOXES			
Glove	$600-750	$850-1500	$1500-3800
Handkerchief	$425-500	$500-900	$900-2200
Puff/Hair	$75-125	$175-275	$300-500
Jewel (round)	$475-600	$650-975	$975-2800
BUTTER			
Covered	$300-475	$525-775	$775-1450
Pat	$25-40	$60-90	$90-130
Tub	$150-225	$250-400	$400-725
Stick/Fluff	$100-175	$200-400	$500-850
CANDLESTICK			
Single 10"	$175-275	$275-525	$525-775
Pair	$375-600	$900-1350	$1500-3600
Candelabrum (single)	$950-1300	$1400-1900	$2000-6500
CARAFES			
Regular	$60-125	$200-350	$450-750
Night Cap	$350-600	$600-900	$1000-2800
CELERY			
Oval	$75-175	$225-350	$350-650
Footed	n/a	$975-1500	$1500-2400
Upright	$200-325	$350-475	$600-850
CHEESE			
Covered	$175-300	$325-650	$650-1100
Cheese & Cracker	$150-225	$250-400	$400-675

	Standard	Choice	Premium
COMPOTES			
Squat	$90-175	$225-350	$400-650
Tall 10"-12"	$250-375	$400-800	$850-1800
Covered	$275-400	$575-1100	$1200-2400
Handled	$175-250	$300-750	$750-1000
Divided	$175-250	$300-750	$750-1000
CORNUCOPIA	$3200-3800	$4000-5400	$5500-7500
DECANTERS			
Wine	$350-900	$1200-1600	$2000-4400
Whiskey 12"	$350-700	$1000-1800	$1800-3800
Handled	$475-900		$1300-1800
	$1800-4000		
Demijohn	$650-975	$1100-1600	$1600-4000
Tantalus (2 bottle)	$1400-2400	$1500-2900	$3000-5500
DISH			
Oval/Round 5"	$75-175	$200-425	$450-1000
Square 8"-9"	$450-750	$800-1200	$1400-2600
Covered dish	n/a	$1400-2200	$2200-3800
Handled	$150-275	$275-400	$400-900
FLOWER HOLDER			
Center 10"	$750-1000	$1100-1600	$1800-3000
Globe 7"	$225-375	$400-700	$700-1500
Canoe 12"	$550-800	$800-1000	$1200-1900
Femer 8"	$125-200	$225-375	$400-750
Violet	$100-125	$150-225	$250-425
Footed Bowl	$275-400	$350-425	$450-800
Pot 6"	$175-250	$275-375	$400-800
GLASSWARE			
Champagne	$25-50	$50-100	$150-350
Claret	$25-40	$50-75	$100-300
Wine	$25-35	$45-70	$100-300
Cordial	$20-30	$40-60	$75-125
Tumbler	$20-30	$45-70	$85-400
Shot	$20-35	$45-70	$85-400
Ale	$40-80	$90-125	$150-350
Sherry	$25-35	$45-75	$100-250
Mug	$150-225	$250-400	$450-850
ICE			
Bowl	$225-425	$450-650	$650-1000
Tub	$200-350	$375-600	$650-900
JARS			
Cracker	$650-1000	$1100-1600	$1800-3800
Tobacco 7"	$800-1200	$1400-2600	$2500-4400
Cigar 8"	$850-1300	$1500-2500	$2600-4400
JUG			
Champagne	$550-775	$800-1400	$1500-3200
Tankard	$275-425	$650-1300	$1300-2200
Footed	$500-675	$700-1400	$1400-2600

	Standard	Choice	Premium
Lemonade	$425-550	$600-900	$900-1500
Bulbous	$625-775	$850-1350	$1400-2100
Silver Trim	$800-1000	$1100-1800	$1800-5000
LAMPS			
Oil 7"-8"	$800-1200	$1200-1900	$1900-2700
Small	$2000-3500	$4000-6500	$7000-12000
Tall	$6500-8500	$8500-14000	$14000-32000
MISCELLANEOUS			
Loving Cup (small)	n/a	$300-500	n/a
Loving Cup (large)	$500-750	$800-1000	$1000-1600
Clock 5"-6"	$450-600	$600-800	$800-1400
Flask 4"	$150-225	$250-400	$400-650
String Box	n/a	$375-675	n/a
Muscilage	n/a	$325-650	n/a
Paperweight	n/a	$375-625	n/a
Toothpick	$40-75	$75-175	$200-1500
NAPPIES			
No Handle 6"	$50-90	$90-150	$200-725
One Handle 6"	$75-100	$125-200	$250-775
Two Handle 7"	$85-125	$150-225	$275-800
Three Handle 5"-6"	$125-200	$250-375	$375-1000
OILS			
Small	$125-175	$200-275	$325-600
Tall	$150-200	$225-400	$400-825
Footed	$225-325	$350-850	$900-2400
PICKLE/RELISH			
Scenic 8"	$275-350	$375-500	$500-800
Handled	$75-125	$150-350	$375-600
Oval	$50-100	$125-375	$350-650
PLATES			
5"-6"	$100-225	$225-375	$375-775
7"-8"	$125-225	$225-400	$425-2800
9"-10"	$200-325	$350-475	$475-2800
POTS			
Tea	$1700-2000	$2000-3200	$3200-6000
Coffee	$2800-3400	$3400-5200	$5200-8800
PUNCH BOWLS			
One Piece 14"	$750-1500	$1500-2300	$2300-4600
Two Piece Tall 14"	$1200-2200	$2200-3800	$3800-6400
Two Piece Squat 12"	$1000-1600	$1600-2600	$2600-5400
Two Piece Small 8"-10"	$1000-1400	$1500-2500	$2500-550
Two Piece Med. 12"-14"	$1400-1800	$1800-3000	$3500-600

	Standard	Choice	Premium
Two Piece Large 15"-18"	$1400-2200	$2500-4000	$4500-10000
SAUCERS			
Round 5"	$75-100	$100-225	$250-800
Handled	$75-100	$100-250	$250-850
SPOONER			
Upright	$125-175	$175-275	$275-675
Footed	$125-175	$200-375	$375-850
Tray	$100-150	$225-350	$350-575
SUGAR & CREAM			
Small	$100-175	$200-300	$325-675
Medium		$150-250	$250-375
$375-750			
Large	$225-300	$300-525	$525-1600
Footed		$250-350	$350-550
$550-2200			
Covered	$250-350	$350-550	$550-2400
Lump Sugar	n/a	$150-525	n/a
Sifter	n/a	$275-550	n/a
SYRUP			
Small (all glass)	$100-175	$175-300	$300-525
Small (silver top)	225-325	$350-475	$500-650
TRAYS			
Bread	$300-400	$400-675	$700-2400
Cake Low Foot	$400-650	$700-825	$900-2800
Cake Tall Footed	$1800-2500	$2500-5500	$5500-10000
Two Piece	$1800-2500	$2500-5500	$5500-10000
Oval 10"-12"	$500-800	$800-1100	$1200-3200
Oval 14"-18"	$800-950	$950-1600	$1600-4400
Rectangle 14"	$700-900	$900-1500	$1500-4400
Round 12"-14"	$700-900	$900-1300	$1300-4200
Handled 6"-8"	$750-950	$1000-1400	$1400-3200
Square 9"	$450-850	$900-1400	$1400-2600
Acorn/Leaf	n/a	$1500-2000	$2000-5200
Shell	n/a	$1500-2000	$2000-5200
VASES			
Small 6"-8"	$100-150	$150-325	$350-950
Medium 10"-14"	$200-525	$550-725	$725-2200
Large 16"-20"	$800-1300	$1400-1850	$2000-4400
Tubular 12"	$200-325	$350-650	$700-2200
Urn	$425-700	$700-1000	$1000-3800
Two Handled 12"	$500-650	$700-1100	$1200-2700
Fan	$500-650	$700-1100	$1200-1500
Hanging w/chain	$475-675	$700-1300	$1400-3000
Shower Five Piece	$1700-3100	$2100-3000	$3000-4800
Epergne 25"-30"	$4500-7500	$7500-14000	$15000-28000

Index of Identified Patterns

Name	Company	Illustration Number
Antoinette #707	Straus	S235
Arlington	Wilcox	S255
Armanda	Hawkes	S93
Aster	Hawkes	S126
Astor	Hawkes	S95
Astoria	Fry	C87
Atlantic	Bergen	C162
Avondale	Unger	S251
Beverly	Meriden	C189
Brilliant	Libbey	S144
Brunswick	Hawkes	P95
Byzantine	Meriden	C190-C191
Cardinal	Maple City	S187
Champion	Quaker City	S223
Chrysanthemum	Hawkes	P96
Chrysanthemum	Parsche	S212
Chrysanthemum	Sinclaire	S226
Clairemont	Unger	P252
Colonial	Bergen	S163
Columbia	Quaker City	C61
Columbus	Hawkes	S97
Columbus	Straus	C236
Concord	Alford	C159
Crescent	Parsche	S213
Criterian	Alford	C160
Cut & Water Cress	Hawkes	C98
Cypress	Clark	C81
Delft Diamond	Hawkes	S99
DeSoto	Bergen	S164-5
Douglas	Bergen	C166
"Drape"	Straus	C237
Ellsmere	Quaker City	S224
English	Hawkes	S100
Enterprise	Bergen	S167
Enterprise	Elmira	C174
Evertt	Higgins & Seiter	S182
Flemish Odel	Clark	P82
Fem	Ohio	P203
Grapes	Tuthill	S246
Henry VIII	Clark	P83
Hexagon Diamond	Mt. Washington	C200
Hob Diamond	Dorflinger	C35
Hobnail	Hawkes	C35
Holland	Hawkes	S101
Hudson	Hawkes	C102
India	Huntly	S183
Iona	Libbey	C145
Gravic Iris	Hawkes	S127
Ivenia	Libbey	S146
Japan	Fry	P90
Jupiter	Hawkes	P103
Jupiter	Sterling	A234
Keystone	Bergen	C168
Kohinoor	Hawkes	C104
Leader	Empire	S176
Leona	Taylor Bros	C243
Lotus	Parsche	C214
Manlius	Hawkes	S105
Marion	Hawkes	S106
Marquis	Hawkes	C79
McCedoz	Hoare	C131
Melrose	Hoare	C132, C133, C134
Mistletoe	Clark	C84, C85
Middlesex	New England	S202
Mona	Hawkes	S107
Montrose	Dorflinger	Cover
Navarre	Hawkes	P108
New Brilliant	Libbey	C147
Newport	Hoare	P135

Name	Company	Illustration Number
Norma	Monroe	C199
Oriental	Hawkes	P109
Panel Star	Libbey	C148
Pansy	Pairpoint	S206
Pears	Missouri Cut Glass	C197
Peerless	Straus	C239
Pennington	Missouri Cut Glass	C198
Persian with pinwheels	Pairpoint	S207
Peru	Pairpoint	S208
Phlox	Tuthill	S247
Poppies	Libbey	S149
Portland	Alford	S161
Pricilla	Quaker City	C225
Primrose	Parsche	S215
Prism	Wilcox	S256
Prudence	Hawkes	C110
Radcliffe	Blackmer	P173
Renwick	Bergen	C169
Rex	Hawkes	C101, C111
Savoy	Meriden, Wilcox	C257
Shirley	Meriden	S192
"Special"	Empire	C177, C178
Star	Hoare	C136
Star	Meriden	P193
Strawberry Diamond	Hoare	C394
Strawberry Diamond	Meriden	S194
Taxi	Fry	C91
(Gravic) Thistle	Hawkes	S125
(Gravic) Tiger Flower	Hawkes	S129
Tokio	Krantz-Smith	C184, C185
Venetian	Straus	P240
Gravic Wild Rose	Hawkes	S130
Willow	Pairpoint	C209
Venus	Bergen	C170
Versailles & Engineering	Sinclaire	S114
Viola	Unger	P253
Waldorf	Taylor Bros.	C244
Winola	Bergen	C171
Zemona	Pitkin & Brooks	C219
Zesta	Pitkin & Brooks	P220
#1	Hawkes	S112
#1	Sinclaire	S227
#4	Sinclaire	C229
#5	Hawkes	S112
#7	Libbey	C150
#55	Libbey	S151
#81	Pairpoint	S210
#99	Dorflinger	C87
#100	Elmira	C175
#124	Hoare	C137
#174	Libbey	S152
#293	Dorflinger	S88
#631	Hoare	C138
#634	P & B	C221
#891	Meriden	S195
#1021	Sinclaire	C230
#1240	Hoare	S140
#1397	Hoare	C139
#1449	Unger	S254
#1946	Hoare	S141
#30194	Hawkes	S113
#4334	Fry	S92
#8505	Meriden	P196
#9254	Oskamp, Nolting	S204
#9497	Oskamp, Nolting	S205
#50334	Fry	S92
#74160	Marshall-Field	C188
#18267	Hawkes	S114

Index of Companies